BOYCOTTS, STRIKES, AND
MARCHES

Protests of the
Civil Rights Era

BARBARA DIGGS

EXPLORE QR CONNECTIONS!

You can use a smartphone or tablet app to scan the QR codes and explore more! Cover up neighboring QR codes to make sure you're scanning the right one. You can find a list of urls on the Resources page.

If the QR code doesn't work, try searching the internet with the Keyword Prompts to find other helpful sources.

🔍 civil rights protests

Nomad Press

A division of Nomad Communications

10 9 8 7 6 5 4 3 2 1

Copyright © 2020 by Nomad Press. All rights reserved.

This book was manufactured by CGB Printers, North Mankato, Minnesota, United States

October 2020, Job #1010677

ISBN Softcover: 978-1-61930-919-7

ISBN Hardcover: 978-1-61930-916-6

Educational Consultant, Marla Conn

Questions regarding the ordering of this book should be addressed to

Nomad Press

2456 Christian St., White River Junction, VT 05001

www.nomadpress.net

Printed in the United States.

Discover the **PASSION** and **CONVICTION** of the **1950s**, **'60s**, and **'70s**!

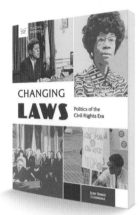

In *Changing Laws: Politics of the Civil Rights Era*, middle graders explore the key legislative and judicial victories of the era that spanned from 1954 to the early 1970s, including *Brown v. Board of Education*, the Civil Rights Act of 1964, the Voting Rights Act of 1965, and the Fair Housing Act of 1968, all of which couldn't have happened without the increased activism of the times. Kids explore how marches, demonstrations, boycotts, and lawsuits prodded local and state governments to reveal the bigotry of their laws and the brutality of their oppression of Black citizens.

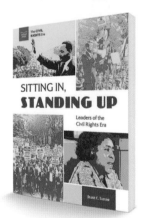

Sitting In, Standing Up: Leaders of the Civil Rights Era tells the story of one of the most tumultuous and important eras in American history through the lives of five major figures of the Civil Rights Movement of the 1950s and 1960s: Thurgood Marshall, Fannie Lou Hamer, Martin Luther King Jr., Ella Baker, and John Lewis. The work of these people sparked the passion of a nation and helped change the tide of social injustice in a way that reverberates to this day.

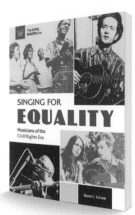

Singing for Equality: Musicians of the Civil Rights Era introduces middle graders to the history of the Civil Rights Movement and explores the vital role that music played in the tumultuous period of American history during the 1950s, '60s, and '70s.

The heart of the Civil Rights Movement beats in the music and musicians of the times, whose work was both an inspiration and a reflection of the changes happening in America and to its people. Bob Dylan, Mavis Staples and the Staple Singers, Nina Simone, Sam Cooke, and James Brown all epitomized the passion and commitment shown by those involved in the movement and portrayed the struggles encountered by an entire race of people with gritty beauty and moving calls to action and thought.

TABLE OF
CONTENTS

A demonstration of mourning and protest after the Triangle Shirtwaist Factory fire of March 25, 1911

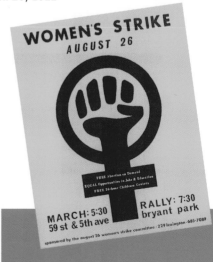

March on
Washington, 1963

Women fight for
their right to vote
in 1913.

Rosa Parks is
arrested for refusing
to give up her seat
to a white person,
1956.

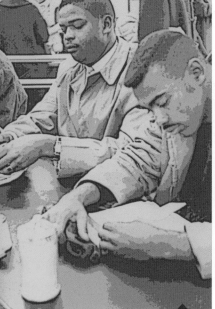

The Woolworth
Sit-In, 1960

The civil rights March on
Washington, DC, 1963

WHAT ARE WE
PROTESTING?

FAST FACTS

WHAT?
The Civil Rights Era was a period when many groups stood up for their rights.

WHY?
People who'd been historically ignored and mistreated, including African Americans, women, and members of the LGBTQ communities, demanded that their civil rights no longer be abused.

WHEN?
From the mid-1950s to early 1970s

HOW?
Through marches, sit-ins, strikes, and boycotts, people across the country worked for equal rights for all.

The Civil Rights Era is a period in American history that began in the mid-1950s and lasted until the early 1970s. During this time, different groups of people fought for the right to be treated equally or to achieve social justice. For many of them, their fight took the form of protest.

1

Many of the rights and privileges Americans enjoy today are a result of the protests that took place during the Civil Rights Era. This was when the Civil Rights Movement erupted across the United States, the protests focused on racism and segregation affecting African Americans. Today, it's illegal to deny people services, housing, jobs, or education because of their skin color. That's a direct result of the Civil Rights Movement. Before then, few people could conceive of an America where such things would be permissible. But thankfully, some people took brave, bold action to help bring about a more equal and just society.

The Montgomery bus boycott, the draft card burning protests of the Vietnam War, the Delano grape strike and boycott, the first Gay Pride March, and the Women's Strike for Equality all took place during the Civil Rights Era. These were important flash points on the path toward true civil rights for everyone.

Have you heard of the Black Lives Matter movement? People across the United States have been marching and protesting unequal treatment of African Americans since the movement began in 2013. But it's not the first time a massive social movement has worked toward change.

The civil rights March on Washington in August 1963 saw about 250,000 people gather to peacefully demand an end to racism.

CIVIL RIGHTS TIMELINE

1954
The U.S. Supreme Court decision *Brown v. Board of Education* rules that segregated schools are unconstitutional.

1957
President Eisenhower sends in federal troops to protect nine Black students as they integrate Central High School in Little Rock, Arkansas.

June 11, 1963
After Alabama Governor George Wallace blocks admission of Black students into the University of Alabama, President Kennedy sends federal troops to maintain order.

CONNECT

Watch a short biography on Rosa Parks. Why do you think she refused to move?

🔍 **PBS Rosa video**

The Pursuit of Happiness

When the United States was first forming as a country, the Founding Fathers provided some direction in terms of the kind of society they thought it could be. In 1776, the Declaration of Independence was drafted to document a place where all people would be granted basic rights, such as "Life, Liberty and the pursuit of Happiness."

However, even the signers of the Declaration weren't completely behind this idea. Many of them owned slaves. The institution of slavery kept an entire race of people oppressed. Slaves were prevented from pursuing happiness. They were not free to live where or with whom they wanted. They were forced to work under harsh conditions and would be beaten or even killed if they displeased their masters. Even after slavery was abolished, Black people faced many obstacles to citizenship, building wealth, and owning land.

Native Americans, too, weren't considered citizens in the new country. Instead, their lands were simply taken. Families were split up with no regard to the traditions and cultures of thousands of years.

June 19, 1964
The Civil Rights Act prohibits segregation in public accommodations.

February 29, 1968
The Kerner Commission report is released and concludes the United States is moving toward two separate and unequal societies—Black and white.

April 11, 1968
In the wake of the assassination of Dr. Martin Luther King Jr., President Johnson pushes Congress to pass the Fair Housing Bill.

November 5, 1968
The election of Richard M. Nixon as president signals a retreat from federal support for major civil rights legislation.

Even after slavery was abolished during the Civil War with the Thirteenth Amendment, Jim Crow laws in the Southern states and other forms of racial discrimination in the Northern states meant that people of color were still barred from the most basic of human rights. These included getting a good education, being considered for good jobs, voting, and simply living in peace. Native Americans, African Americans, gay and transgender people, and women were all treated unfairly during this time. If you weren't a white man, you had fewer rights.

America's Tradition of Protest

Civil Rights Era protests are remembered for their breadth, power, and success. Still, it wasn't the first time in American history that people used acts of dissent to express dissatisfaction with society. In fact, the country might still be under English rule if American colonizers had not protested British laws and policies they believed to be unfair. Protests such as the Boston Tea Party and the boycott of British goods helped give the colonists courage and determination to start the American Revolution.

The founders of the United States believed that the right to protest was so crucial to a free and fair society that they ensured citizens of this right in the First Amendment of the U.S. Constitution. Since then, millions of Americans have used the First Amendment's protections to protest state and federal laws and social injustice with the hope of bringing about change.

Word Power!

This book is packed with lots of new vocabulary! Try figuring out the meanings of unfamiliar words using the context and roots of the words. There is a glossary in the back to help you and Word Power check-ins for every chapter.

A 1973 set of four stamps showing the Boston Tea Party. The protesting colonists were dressed as Native Americans.

Many protests prior to the Civil Rights Era brought significant changes to laws and policies that we still benefit from today. On April 5, 1911, 120,000 people marched in New York City after 146 workers died in a fire at the Triangle Shirtwaist Factory due to unsafe working conditions. The demonstration helped bring national attention to the issue, resulting in stronger labor unions and, eventually, better wages, labor laws, and safety reforms.

On March 3, 1913, the day before the presidential inauguration of Woodrow Wilson, some 8,000 women marched down Pennsylvania Avenue in Washington, DC, calling for a constitutional amendment granting women the right to vote. Although it took seven years, the U.S. Congress passed the Nineteenth Amendment granting women suffrage in 1920. Many historians credit this protest with creating the spark and momentum that led to change.

With such a legacy of successful protests and the assurances of the First Amendment, it is not surprising that oppressed or marginalized people during the Civil Rights Era turned toward protest as a means to make their voices heard and push for change.

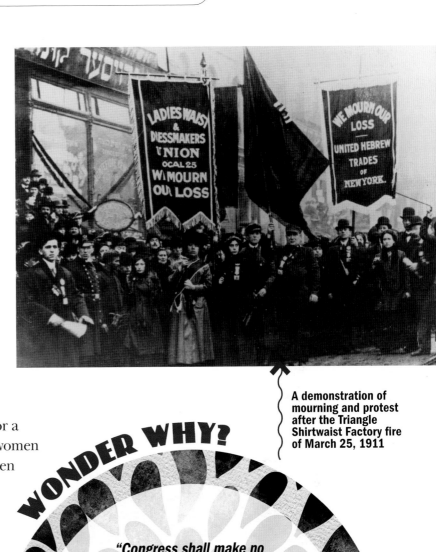

A demonstration of mourning and protest after the Triangle Shirtwaist Factory fire of March 25, 1911

WONDER WHY?

"Congress shall make no law . . . abridging the freedom of speech . . . or the right of people to peaceably assemble, and petition the government for a redress of their grievances."

Why do you think the Founding Fathers put freedom of speech and the right to peaceably assemble together in the First Amendment?

Civil Rights Era Protests

You might be wondering: If Americans have been protesting for hundreds of years, what was the big deal about the Civil Rights Era protests? Quite a few things.

One factor was the sheer number of protests. Within the era's 20-year span, there were thousands of organized protests, all across the country. At first, these protests were mainly concentrated in the South as African Americans fought segregation and racial discrimination. But as an increasing number of people found their voices, acts of protest found their way to hundreds of cities and towns, touching every single state in the nation.

Suffragists march to gain the right to vote in 1913.

EARLY ACTIVISTS

An activist is a person who tries to influence and change social or legal causes through protest. Although the term is fairly modern, many people in eighteenth- and nineteenth-century America would be labeled "activists" if they were alive today. One early activist was David Ruggles (1810–1849), an African American who lived in New York City during the 1820s. Ruggles openly engaged in antislavery activities, including speaking out against the institution, writing and circulating anti-slavery pamphlets, opening an anti-slavery bookstore, and helping enslaved people escape to freedom. What else did people do to protest slavery?

CONNECT

You can learn more about Ruggles and other early American social activists at this website.

 David Ruggles

Another factor was the range of issues people protested. The Civil Rights Movement's battle to end racial discrimination was the most prominent. Still, many other groups, often inspired by the civil rights activists' success, also began to organize to express their discontent with unfair treatment or situations.

Women began speaking out about not having rights equal to men. Young men objected to being sent to fight in a war they believed was unjust. Native Americans protested the United States's failure to honor a federal treaty that promised to return Native lands by taking over Alcatraz Island, a former California prison. For many people, it was clear that life in America could not proceed as it had before.

Civil Rights Era protests were also memorable because they were remarkably effective. People saw in real-time the extraordinary power groups had when they banded together and remained committed to their cause. As the world watched, laws and customs that had seemed engraved in stone crumbled beneath the unshakeable persistence of activists and allies.

Even when protests did not result in social or legal change, they often brought attention to issues that many people had never considered before. Sometimes, the protests inspired individuals to change their habits, customs, or ideas.

WONDER WHY?

What were some of the other major protests around the world during the early twentieth century? Were people protesting issues similar to those in the United States?

The Form of Protest

When you hear the word "protest," what picture comes to mind? Most people probably think of a large group of people marching with signs and banners with slogans on them. But there are hundreds of different manners of protest. Sometimes, protest can be an action, such as a march or a demonstration. Other times, it can be an absence of action, such as refusing to go to work or buy certain products.

Protest also can be represented through art, such as sculptures or songs. It can take the form of civil disobedience, when people break laws they believe to be unfair or immoral. It can also be a symbolic act. Some forms of protests include violence—against oneself or others—or the destruction of property, such as the Boston Tea Party. There is debate over the effectiveness of these types of protest. And they are not protected by the First Amendment.

Black activists protested segregation by sitting and reading in a space reserved for whites during the Woolworth Sit-In in Durham, North Carolina, 1960.

WONDER WHY?

Why might peaceful protests be more effective than violent protests? Is violence ever more powerful than peaceful action?

March on Washington, DC, 1963
Credit: Marion S. Trikosko

During the Civil Rights Era, people used every single one of these forms of protest and more to bring attention to their causes and challenge the status quo.

While protesting might sound easy, it was not. Activists frequently suffered serious consequences from engaging in protests. Tens of thousands of activists landed in jail for their actions. Some became estranged from their families and communities. Other lost their jobs.

Many were jeered at, harassed, or even physically assaulted by those who disagreed with them.

"I would like to be remembered as a person who wanted to be free . . . so other people would be also free."
Rosa Parks (1913–2005), civil rights activist

A RIGHT WAY TO PROTEST?

Do you think there's a right or wrong way to protest? Former football player Colin Kaepernick (1987-) lost his position as quarterback for the San Francisco 49ers after many people felt it was inappropriate for him to protest police brutality and racism by kneeling during the national anthem. What do you think of his choice of protest? Do you think it was effective? Why or why not?

In the most extreme cases, protestors such as Dr. Martin Luther King Jr. (1929–1968) and Medgar Evers (1925–1965) were assassinated, or murdered, for their actions. Why do you think people continued to protest in the face of such hardships?

Ground-Breaking Protests

Despite its turmoil and division, the Civil Rights Era was a fascinating period. Society was undergoing a significant upheaval right before everyone's eyes. For the first time, many people pushed to the fringes of society found a way to make their voices heard. But it took a great deal of effort, risk, determination, and commitment to get to that point.

In this book, you'll get to know five different protests from this legendary period. You'll learn how these protests came about, the people involved, the groups affected, and the societal and legal changes they brought. You'll also learn to identify the elements of a successful protest, how to analyze contemporary protests, and even how to organize a demonstration of your own. Get ready to see protests, all around the world, in a whole new light!

"The fight is never about grapes or lettuce. It is always about people."

Cesar Chavez (1927–1993), labor leader and organizer of the Delano grape strike

A poster for the first Women's Strike for Equality in 1970

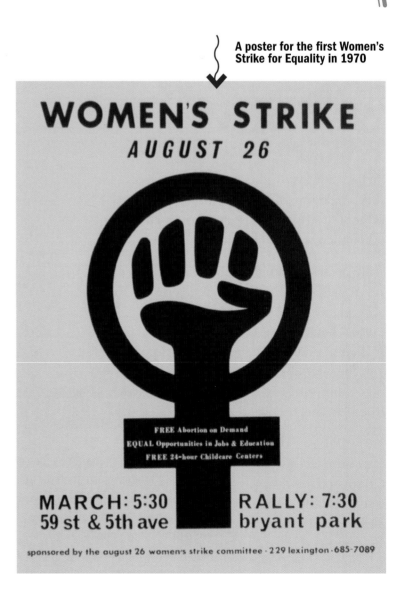

WOMEN'S STRIKE

AUGUST 26

FREE Abortion on Demand
EQUAL Opportunities in Jobs & Education
FREE 24-hour Childcare Centers

MARCH: 5:30
59 st & 5th ave

RALLY: 7:30
bryant park

sponsored by the august 26 women's strike committee · 229 lexington · 685-7089

PROJECT

Planning a Boycott

Segregated buses and trains were only one of the ways whites discriminated against African Americans in the Jim Crow South. A boycott is the act of refusing to buy, use, or participate in something as a form of protest. What are some potential advantages and challenges of a boycott?"

☮ **Imagine that you wanted to protest these discriminatory policies and laws.** Which ones might be the best to protest through boycott? For each one, explain why you think a boycott might effective.

Research the other ways in which African Americans were discriminated against during the Jim Crow era.

🔍 **examples of Jim Crow laws**

☮ **Now choose one law that you think could be protested by boycott and create a detailed outline for organizing the boycott.** In doing this, consider the following:

- The goal of the boycott
- How the boycott would pressure the boycott target
- How you would gather support for the boycott
- The potential financial costs of the boycott

- How to spread news of the boycott
- How you could keep people interested in the boycott

CONNECT

Can someone who has never experienced or witnessed racism learn about it? In the 1960s, a teacher named Jane Elliot developed a method to do this based on eye color. Read an article and watch a video about her teachings at this website.

🔍 **People Jane Elliot**

☮ **Create a list of demands for the boycott target.** What would you want it to do? What would make you end the boycott?

TEXT TO WORLD Have you ever been to a march or protest? What was it like?

Rosa Parks is fingerprinted on February 22, 1956, after being arrested as part of the boycott.

CHAPTER ONE

THE MONTGOMERY
BUS BOYCOTT

**F
A
S
T
F
A
C
T
S**

WHAT?
The Montgomery bus boycott in Montgomery, Alabama

WHY?
To end racial segregation in public transportation

WHEN?
December 5, 1955–December 20, 1956

HOW?
African American bus riders from around Montgomery, Alabama, refused to ride the buses until their demands for fair treatment and representation were met. They organized car pools and taxi services, fundraised, and kept their boycott peaceful.

The Montgomery bus boycott is widely considered to be the protest that kicked off the entire Civil Rights Era. And what a start it was! The protest involved the entire African American community in Montgomery, Alabama, and caught the attention of the whole nation as it lasted more than a year. Most important, it was an unequivocal success.

This boycott isn't important just because it led to the end of legal racial segregation in public transport, but also because the protestors' peaceful-yet-determined actions had a ripple effect throughout the country. Once people saw how effective nonviolent protest could be, countless others were motivated to initiate similar protests to bring change to other unjust conditions.

Let's take a look at why this particular protest was so extraordinary.

Segregation in the American South

You might already know the basics of the Montgomery boycott: Rosa Parks, an African American woman, was arrested for refusing to give up her seat on a bus for a white man, triggering a city-wide bus boycott among African Americans.

Sounds simple, right? In reality, the boycott involved a great deal of risks, sacrifice, planning, and danger.

An African American man drinks at a "colored" water fountain in Oklahoma, 1939

Credit: Russel Lee

CIVIL RIGHTS TIMELINE

December 1, 1955
Rosa Parks is arrested for refusing to give up her seat to a white passenger.

December 5, 1955
About 90 to 100 percent of the black community participate in the boycott.

December 5, 1955
The Montgomery Improvement Association is created, with Martin Luther King Jr. as its president.

The story begins nearly 80 years earlier, in the mid-1880s, when many Southern states began to pass racist laws demanding that African Americans and whites remain segregated in almost all public spaces. These "Jim Crow" laws forced African Americans to sit in the "colored" sections of restaurants, movie theaters, trains, and buses. The laws also prevented these citizens from attending the same schools, swim in the same pools, or even drink from the same water fountain as whites.

The purpose of these laws wasn't merely to keep African Americans and whites separate, but also to give whites special privileges and keep Blacks in an inferior position in society. Why do you think this system lasted so long?

JIM CROW

Jim Crow laws got their strange name because of a white minstrel performer named Thomas Dartmouth Rice (1808-1860), who, in the 1820s, dressed in blackface to sing and dance and make fun of enslaved African Americans. Rice called his blackface character "Jim Crow," and this quickly grew into a derogatory name for black people and soon became the term used to describe racist laws. These laws were meant to legitimize the system of racism and the relegation of African Americans as second-class citizens.

December 8, 1955
The MIA issues a formal list of demands, which the city refuses.

January 30, 1956
Dr. King's home is bombed. Dr. King calls for peaceful protest rather than violent action.

June 5, 1956
A federal district court rules that bus segregation is unconstitutional.

December 21, 1956
Montgomery's buses are officially desegregated and the boycott ends.

Resistance Against Segregation

Of course, African Americans detested these cruel and humiliating laws. Yet it was dangerous for anyone to resist or protest. If they did, they could be thrown into jail, fined, or become the target of white retaliation and violence. When a Black person tried to claim the same rights as a white person, it was called, "stepping over their color line."

White supremacy groups such as the Ku Klux Klan regularly threatened, beat, and even killed Black people who tried to stand up for themselves. Even regular white citizens felt free to put Black people "in their place" through violence or humiliation. Because the police forces, courts, and juries were always composed of white people, white citizens knew they were unlikely to suffer any consequences from their actions.

Because resisting could bring such severe consequences, there were few major organized protests of segregation before 1955. Instead, African Americans fought racist laws through the federal court system with the help of the National Association for the Advancement of Colored People (NAACP). This multiracial organization was created in 1909 to achieve justice for Black people. It spent decades challenging the constitutionality of laws that segregated public schools and universities.

The group's efforts paid off. In 1954, the U.S. Supreme Court ruled that segregated schools were unconstitutional in the case of *Brown v. Board of Education*.

African Americans and others celebrated all across the country. But much of white society wasn't about to let go of segregation so easily. For most people in the South, life continued as usual.

Enter Rosa Parks

On Thursday, December 1, 1955, Rosa Parks boarded a bus in Montgomery, Alabama, after a long day at work. Alabama law required Black people to sit at the back of city buses, even if there were seats available in the white section. So, Parks, a seamstress, headed to the back and sat in the first row of the colored section.

COLORED
WAITING ROOM

PRIVATE PROPERTY
NO PARKING
Driving through or Turning Around

**At the bus station in Durham,
North Carolina, May 1940**

Credit: Jack Delano, Farm Security Administration—Office of
War Information Photograph Collection (Library of Congress)

WHEN IS A LAW "UNCONSTITUTIONAL"?

The U.S. Constitution is a set of laws that the entire country must follow. If a state law permits an act that the Constitution forbids, then a federal court may declare the state law "unconstitutional" and, therefore, invalid.

The men who wrote the U.S. Constitution couldn't anticipate what life would be like in the future and what laws might be needed to keep society functioning as well as possible, so certain lawyers study constitutional law and act as interpreters. When questions come up over whether a law is constitutional or not, these lawyers present their thoughts and conclusions to help judges make decisions.

Shortly afterward, the bus driver stopped the bus and told Parks and three other African Americans that because the bus was full, they had to give up their seats to accommodate a white man who wanted to sit. No Black people were allowed even to sit in the same row as a white person! Three people obeyed the bus driver and got up.

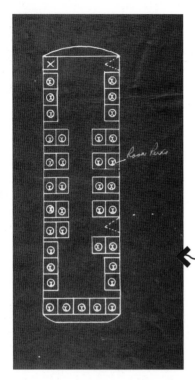

A diagram of where Parks was sitting on the bus

Parks stayed where she was.

At that time, Parks was 42 years old. She had lived under Jim Crow laws her entire life—and hated it. Even before this fateful bus ride, she was a fierce activist committed to fighting segregation and other racial injustices. She had been the secretary of the Montgomery NAACP chapter for 12 years and had organized the local NAACP Youth Council.

Moreover, she was not afraid to break segregation laws. In fact, the very same bus driver had ejected her from a bus more than 10 years earlier for refusing to sit in the "colored" section.

When Parks refused to move, the bus driver called the police. She was quickly arrested and jailed.

A Whirlwind Weekend

CLAUDETTE COLVIN

Many people don't realize that Rosa Parks wasn't the first person to refuse to give up her seat for a white person on a bus. Just nine months before Parks made her stance, Claudette Colvin (1939–), a 15-year-old student in Montgomery, also refused to stand for a white passenger. She was arrested, handcuffed, and forcibly removed from the bus. At first, NAACP members wanted to use her arrest to test the constitutionality of the segregation laws. But they became less enthusiastic when they realized that Colvin was pregnant. Why did this make a difference? Why was Rosa Parks considered a better rallying figure for the desegregation cause? Is that fair?

Word of Parks's arrest spread like a blaze through the Black community in Montgomery. She was a well-known and respected person. The news soon reached the ears of E.D. Nixon (1899–1987), the president of the local NAACP chapter. Nixon had worked with Parks for years and quickly posted bail for her so she could go home.

News of the arrest also reached members of the Women's Political Council (WPC).

Henry L. Moon, Roy Wilkins, Herbert Hill, and Thurgood Marshall, leaders of the NAACP in 1956

Credit: Al Ravenna, *New York World-Telegram* and the *Sun* staff photographer

This local organization was composed of professional Black women who worked to fight discrimination and increase civic involvement in the African American community.

The WPC had long been fed up with the bus system's racist policies. About 18 months before Parks's arrest, members had met with Montgomery's mayor to discuss changes to these unfair practices.

For example, they wanted to stop the company's policy of forcing African Americans to stand over empty "white" seats when all the places in the "colored" section were full. They also wanted the bus company to allow Blacks to enter at the front of the bus. When the city refused to meet these demands, the WPC began seriously considering a bus boycott.

The outrage of Parks's arrest galvanized them into immediate action.

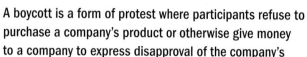

WHAT IS A BOYCOTT?

A boycott is a form of protest where participants refuse to purchase a company's product or otherwise give money to a company to express disapproval of the company's actions or its position on a social or political issue. The idea is that if the company loses enough profit, it'll change its action or stance. The first bus boycott against segregation occurred in Baton Rouge, Louisiana, in 1953.

CONNECT

Read more about the Baton Rouge boycott at this website. Why do you think this bus boycott is largely forgotten? What might have been different about the Montgomery boycott?

🔍 **NPR first bus boycott**

Nixon and King gathered the ministers and civic leaders of Montgomery to meet on Friday, December 2, to discuss the boycott. Virtually all the leaders of the community attended, and excitement was bubbling over. They talked late into the night about how the boycott should proceed and how long it should last. They decided to call a mass meeting on the evening of the boycott to determine the community's enthusiasm for continuing it.

That night, WPC President Jo Ann Robinson (1912–1992) called E.D. Nixon to discuss the boycott idea. Nixon was enthusiastic and agreed to organize it. They would waste no time—the one-day boycott would take place on Monday, December 5, the same day as Parks's court date.

The WPC leapt into action, copying some 50,000 leaflets announcing the boycott to the African American community. Meanwhile, Nixon called a young, then-little-known minister named Martin Luther King Jr. to ask for his support and help in rallying other community leaders, particularly the ministers of local Black churches. King quickly agreed.

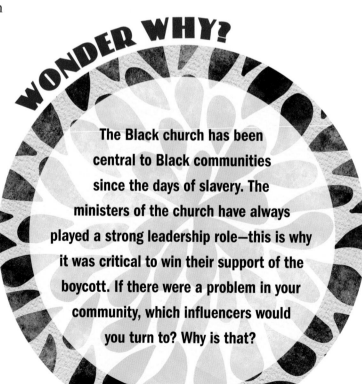

WONDER WHY?

The Black church has been central to Black communities since the days of slavery. The ministers of the church have always played a strong leadership role—this is why it was critical to win their support of the boycott. If there were a problem in your community, which influencers would you turn to? Why is that?

Boycott Begins!

On the morning of the boycott, Dr. King and his wife, Coretta (1927–2006), awoke early. They wanted to catch a glimpse of the first bus of the day in their neighborhood.

Black people made up 70 percent of the bus riders in Montgomery. The majority of the Black community needed to participate in the boycott, otherwise the protest would have no financial impact on the bus company, which would then have no motivation to desegregate.

CONNECT

Listen to a podcast episode about the WPC's role in the bus boycott. Why do you think its members' actions aren't as well-known as those of Rosa Parks and Martin Luther King Jr.?

 news Berkeley Jo Ann Robinson

King was drinking a cup of coffee when Coretta called to him excitedly—the first bus had passed by their home and not a single person was on it! They were elated. The bus was usually packed with African Americans on their way to work. The next few buses were the same—either no people on it or just a few white passengers.

The sidewalks were filled with African Americans walking to work and school that day, pride evident in their stride. Some people rode bikes. Some took taxis (Black-owned taxi companies carried boycotters for the price of a bus fare), while others hitchhiked. A few people even traveled by mule or horse and buggy.

Spirits were high. Groups gathered at bus stops to cheer at the near-empty buses. About 90 percent of the African American population boycotted the buses.

That evening, more than 4,000 jubilant people showed up for the mass meeting at Holt Street Baptist Church, eager to continue what they had begun. King delivered a rousing speech, asking the crowd if they were willing to continue the boycott and keep it nonviolent. The crowd thunderously agreed.

> "There is nothing more majestic than the determined courage of individuals willing to suffer and sacrifice for their freedom and dignity."
>
> Martin Luther King Jr.

Keeping It Going

The bus boycott promised to be huge. More than 17,000 African Americans were daily bus riders in Montgomery. On the evening of the boycott, local leaders formed the Montgomery Improvement Association (MIA) to take charge of the campaign's direction.

WONDER WHY?

Why were people so happy to protest, despite the great inconvenience to them?

A few days after the boycott began, the MIA's executive committee, headed by Dr. King, sent a list of three simple demands to the city commissioners and bus company officials. The leaders wanted first-come, first-served seating on buses, bus drivers to treat Black people courteously, and the bus company to employ Black bus drivers.

City and bus officials met with the MIA, but the talks fell apart quickly.

The MIA knew then that the boycott would last indefinitely. Leaders quickly turned their attention to how to keep the boycott going. Having alternate forms of transportation was crucial to the success of the boycott. If people missed work or were late for their jobs, the protest would be impossible to sustain.

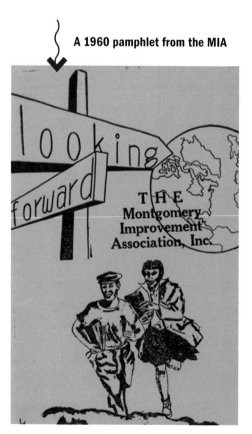

A 1960 pamphlet from the MIA

On the first day of the boycott, Rosa Parks was found guilty of violating the segregation law. She was fined $10 ($116 in today's dollars).

Rosa Parks and others at an event after the boycott

The women of the WPC took charge of coordinating dozens of carpools to get people to work on time. Hundreds of Black people—and even a few whites—volunteered to drive. Other people volunteered to help organize the dispatching of the cars, which took an incredible amount of well-timed coordination. Within a week of the start of the boycott, there were more than 40 carpool dispatch and drop-off points around Montgomery.

Supporting the Boycott

Countless people lent their talents and resources however they could to keep the boycott alive. The Black owner of a large parking lot volunteered his space as the primary dispatch and pick-up station for carpools. An African American pharmacist acted as a dispatcher from his office, filling prescriptions even as he coordinated rides. Musicians led people in inspirational songs before boycott meetings to keep spirits high.

As the unwavering determination of the people of Montgomery captured the attention of the nation and the world, hundreds of thousands of dollars in donations poured into the MIA from all corners. A vast amount of money came from U.S. churches, both Black and white, many of them donating shoes for the walkers in addition to money. Supporters of the NAACP also opened their wallets.

The money allowed the boycott to continue, which in turn caused the bus company to lose between 30,000 and 40,000 fares per day. Eventually, the company had to reduce the number of buses serving Montgomery and raise the fare from 10 to 15 cents.

But it still would not meet the MIA's demands.

White Reaction

Unsurprisingly, the boycott angered many people in the white community. Some protesters were attacked while walking. The cars of Black carpool drivers were vandalized.

WONDER WHY?

The protest cost about $5,000 (about $48,000 today) a month. What kinds of expenses do you think the boycott generated? What did they need to pay for?

But much of the money came from tens of thousands of ordinary individuals from around the world who were disgusted by the injustices of the Jim Crow laws and wanted to support the protestors. With these funds, the MIA was able to hire a full-time secretary, establish a transportation office, and cover many other expenses.

THE CLUB FROM NOWHERE

Georgia Gilmore (1920–1970), an African American cook, formed a cooking club called "The Club from Nowhere" to raise money for the boycott. Gilmore, who had refused to ride buses years earlier after suffering a humiliating experience, cooked and sold hundreds of meals and baked goods each week at local Black businesses and out of private homes. All the funds earned went directly to the MIA. Members of the cooking club remained largely anonymous so they would not be fired from their jobs or suffer retaliation from the white community.

CONNECT

You can read more about Gilmore in this article. Where did the name of the club come from? How did the name of the club show the kind of ingenuity African Americans were forced to adopt in their struggle for equal rights?

Atlas Obscura funded civil rights

The police harassed and arrested carpool drivers for trivial or imaginary traffic violations. They also issued fines to any taxi driver who charged a rate lower than the regular 45-cent fare.

The white supremacist group, the White Citizens Council, doubled in size during the boycott. White supremacists firebombed the homes of Martin Luther King and E.D. Nixon, as well as four Black churches. Fortunately, no one was hurt.

In February 1956, 89 members of the MIA, including King, were arrested for violating a 1921 state law that prohibited acts that "interfered with lawful businesses." Dr. King was the sole person brought to trial. He was found guilty and spent two weeks in jail.

But there was some white support for the boycott. White housewives often drove their Black maids to and from work—some out of support for the cause, many because they didn't want to have to do the housework on their own. Other white people helped the boycotters by driving, making donations, or even boycotting buses themselves.

Rosa Parks, c. 1978
Credit: Judith Sedwick

The U.S. Supreme Court Rules

While the protestors were putting pressure on the bus company through the boycott, the city was under legal pressure. Fred Gray (1930–), a Black lawyer and member of the MIA, brought a suit challenging the constitutionality of the city's segregated bus laws. He filed on behalf of four Black women who had been discriminated against or mistreated on buses because of their race.

Gray argued that the law violated the women's rights to equal protection of the law guaranteed by the Fourteenth Amendment, as in *Brown v. Board*. The lower court agreed with the plaintiffs, but the city appealed to the U.S. Supreme Court.

WONDER WHY?

The four women bringing the lawsuit (the plaintiffs) were Aurelia Browder (1919–1971), Claudette Colvin, Susie McDonald (unknown), and Mary Louise Smith (1937–). Why wasn't Rosa Parks included as a plaintiff? Because of legal technicalities that might have gotten the case stuck in state rather than federal court.

"My resistance to being mistreated on the buses and anywhere else was just a regular thing with me and not just that day."

Rosa Parks

On November 13, 1956, the U.S. Supreme Court ruled that it agreed with the lower court—segregation on public buses and other transportation was unconstitutional. African Americans and people all over the world were ecstatic. After nearly 80 years of extreme oppression, following centuries of slavery, segregation was beginning to crumble at last.

Rosa Parks, 43, sits in the front of a city bus on December 21, 1956, as the U.S. Supreme Court ruling that banned segregation on the city's public transit vehicles takes effect.

The first African American U.S. president, Barack Obama, sits on the famous bus at the Henry Ford Museum, 2012.

Credit: Official White House Photo by Pete Souza

After 381 days of protest, the bus boycott ended on December 20, 1956, when Montgomery officially changed its segregated transportation laws. Although there was still much work to be done in changing racist laws—and racist customs—the success of the bus boycott helped show the country the extraordinary power of a well-organized protest.

The era of protest was just getting started.

The bus on which the protest began, now housed in a museum

PROJECT

Create a Boycott Journal

Pretend it's 1955 and you're an African American student participating in the boycott. Write a diary entry for three different months: December 1955, March 1956, and December 1956.

 In your journal, consider issues such as the following:

- Your feelings about the boycott at the different points in time

- Your hopes and fears about the future of segregation

- What other actions you might take to support the boycott

- How the adults around you might be feeling or acting

CONNECT

To hear firsthand accounts of the Montgomery bus boycott, watch an excerpt from the documentary *Eyes on the Prize*. How do personal accounts help us understand history in a different way?

🔍 **Eyes on Prize part 1**

What vocabulary words did you discover? Can you figure out the meanings of these words? Look in the glossary for help!

blackface, derogatory, galvanize, NAACP, nonviolent protest, retaliation, and sustain

TEXT TO WORLD

Does your family make decisions about what to buy and where to go and how to travel based on making the world a more equal and just place?

A man burns his draft card at an anti-draft demonstration at the Selective Service System headquarters, Washington, DC, 1970.

Credit: *U.S. News & World Report* magazine collection

CHAPTER TWO

VIETNAM WAR

DRAFT RESISTANCE

FASTFACTS

WHAT?
Draft card burning or turn-in, a symbolic protest

WHY?
To end military conscription

WHEN?
1963–1975

HOW?
Men eligible for the draft resisted going to the Vietnam War through a variety of nonviolent methods, including symbolically burning draft cards, moving to different countries, or claiming they are conscientious objectors.

As the battle for civil rights continued with boycotts, sit-ins, and marches, national tensions grew further strained as the United States entered the war in Vietnam. Many Americans found this war morally wrong. When the government began using the draft to call hundreds of thousands of young men to fight, another massive protest movement was born.

For Americans, the Vietnam War began in 1955 after communist Vietnamese forces successfully revolted against the French colonizers who had ruled their country for nearly 80 years. The communists took control over the northern half of Vietnam, while the French yielded power to non-communist Vietnamese in the south. The communists announced their intention to unify the entire country under one government.

The U.S. government feared a fully communist Vietnam. In the decade earlier, the communist Soviet Union had led several Eastern European countries, China, and North Korea to adopt communist totalitarian regimes. The United States worried that if Vietnam also fell to communism, it would greatly increase the power of the Soviet Union and threaten the democratic, capitalist, American way of life.

The United States began to funnel military leaders, equipment, and millions of dollars to the South Vietnamese government to help fight the communist forces. After a decade of such support, the communists continued to make headway.

U.S. soldiers in Vietnam
Credit: manhhai (CC BY 2.0)

In 1965, President Lyndon Johnson (1908–1973) decided to send 3,500 American ground combat troops to Vietnam to help the South Vietnamese military.

CIVIL RIGHTS TIMELINE

1955
The United States begins to send troops, equipment, and money to the South Vietnamese government to help fight communist forces.

December 1963
Eugene Keyes sets his draft card on fire in a statement of peace.

October 15, 1965
David Miller burns his draft card in violation of the Draft Card Mutilation Act and serves 22 months in prison.

October 21, 1967
About 100,000 anti-war protesters gather at the Lincoln Memorial.

COMMUNISM EXPLAINED

What is communism? Communism is an economic system where individuals do not own businesses, land, or factories. In theory, citizens own all things collectively and share the wealth that is produced. In reality, the government runs everything. Communist countries are usually run by dictators who have absolute power over the country and its people and who threaten or punish people who object in any way.

Hawks vs. Doves

Americans were divided about the United States's involvement in the Vietnam war. People who supported it were called "hawks." They feared the spread of communism and believed that national security was at stake. Hawks also thought that Americans should always support their government's foreign policy and that failing to do so was unpatriotic.

This number would grow to 200,000 by the end of the year, then to 385,000 in 1966. By the time the United States ended its involvement in the war in 1972, 2.7 million American soldiers had served in the conflict.

November 1967
Under the draft system, as many as 40,000 young men are called into service each month.

March 25, 1967
Martin Luther King Jr. gives a speech condemning the Vietnam War, pointing out that African Americans are disproportionately affected.

January 1969
The draft system is changed to a lottery system to make the outcomes fairer.

January 1973
The draft is formally ended.

"Doves" were those who objected to American involvement in the war. Some were pacifists who opposed all violence. Others believed that Vietnam had the right to choose its own government, even a communist one, without U.S. interference. They were horrified that the United States was amplifying the death, devastation, and displacement in Vietnam.

Anti-war protests, sit-ins, and marches began to sprout up around the country in 1963. Most demonstrations protested U.S. involvement in the war in general. But, as the government sent more and more men to fight, protests increasingly focused on the draft.

Dreaded Draft

The draft, formally called "conscription," is when the U.S. government demands that American men enlist in the military. During the 1950s and '60s, the Universal Military Training and Service Act required all male U.S. citizens and residents between the ages of 18 and 26 to register with the Selective Service System (SSS). This agency maintains a database containing the personal information of draft-age men.

THE SELECTIVE SERVICE SYSTEM

All male Americans and resident immigrants are still legally required to register with the SSS within 30 days of turning 18. But don't worry! The government maintains this database only in case of an emergency military shortfall. The military is currently an all-volunteer body with enough members to meet its needs.

CONNECT

Watch footage of Vietnam War protests at this website. Have you ever been to an anti-war protest? How are these different from protests that happen today?

 Anti-War Demonstration NYC archive

Every month, even during peacetime, the government would select a number of men from this database to be assessed by their local draft board for their fitness for active military service. Those men considered fit were assigned to a branch of the military and given a job.

Early in the war, the government drafted about 6,000 to 9,000 men per month. As the United States grew more entangled in the conflict, those numbers shot up to 35,000 men per month—and then rose even higher. Approximately 1.7 million drafted men served in Vietnam. That's approximately 25 percent of all who served.

More than 58,000 American soldiers and an estimated 3 million Vietnamese soldiers and citizens were killed in the Vietnam War.

Many young men were gripped with apprehension— especially those who felt the war was morally wrong. Was it their responsibility as an American to blindly answer the call of their country? Was it right to fight in a war they deeply opposed?

For many, the answer was no.

Anti-Vietnam War protesters

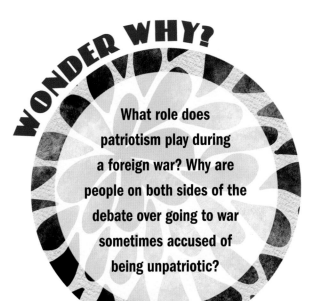

WONDER WHY?

What role does patriotism play during a foreign war? Why are people on both sides of the debate over going to war sometimes accused of being unpatriotic?

A Small Start

Draft resistance began with a single person. On Christmas Eve in 1963, 22-year-old Eugene Keyes (1941–) of Champlain, Illinois, set his draft card on fire and used it to light a candle for "peace on earth." He later refused to report for induction and served a year in jail. Keyes's small act would eventually trigger a huge symbolic protest that became iconic of the Vietnam War era.

As the war heated up, dozens of young men began burning their draft cards in protest. In August 1965, Congress passed a law called the Draft Card Mutilation Act. Under this law, anyone who knowingly destroyed or mutilated their card risked receiving up to five years in prison or a $10,000 fine.

Although the new law may have deterred some draft resisters, it made others become even more determined to protest. Why might that be?

Men were required to carry draft cards with them at all times to prove they had registered with the SSS.

The drawing of draft numbers, 1970

WONDER WHY?

In 2019, a federal judge ruled that excluding women from the SSS registration requirement is unconstitutional. Do you think that women will ever be compelled to register? Why or why not?

Burn, Baby, Burn

In 1965, anti-war activists became increasingly focused on protesting the draft. Most resisters were young, white, male college students who belonged to anti-war groups at their schools or to chapters of larger peace organizations. Many had been involved in the Civil Rights Movement and were committed to nonviolent protest.

WONDER WHY?

Burning a draft card did not prevent a man from being drafted. The protest was only symbolic. Why do you think Congress made burning a draft card illegal anyway? What is burning a draft card symbolic of?

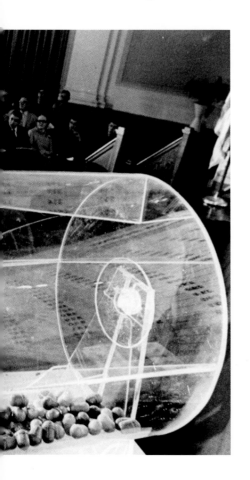

The Draft Card Mutilation Act had raised the stakes for draft resisters. Burning a draft card was no longer a merely symbolic gesture, but also one that held the risk of paying a high price. Neither the public nor the draft card burner himself could take the act lightly.

"I hold allegiance to one thing higher than the government of the United States, and that is my own conscience."

Howard Zinn (1922–2010), historian and anti-war protester

An anti-war protest in 1967, San Francisco, California

Draft resisters often carefully planned card burning events and publicized them in advance. On the chosen date, many took care to dress and style their hair neatly. They'd explain to the crowd why they were protesting the draft or war and then light their cards.

With the stakes so high, what did draft resisters hope to gain by burning their cards? For one, they hoped the act would communicate their horror at what they considered a deeply immoral action by the U.S. government and their refusal to condone or participate in it.

They also hoped that others would be encouraged to join the anti-war movement and help call for the war's end. The idea was that if enough people started burning draft cards, the legal system would be too overwhelmed to punish them all.

But as draft calls continued, resisters realized there was another reason to protest the draft—the draft system was tremendously unfair.

 DAVID MILLER

On October 15, 1965, David Miller (1943–) burned his draft card at an anti-war rally in New York City, making him the first person to publicly violate the Draft Card Mutilation Act. He was arrested by the FBI, tried, and convicted. Miller served 22 months in federal prison.

"A Working-Class War"

Although the majority of the draft resisters were white, middle-class college students, the vast majority of draftees sent to Vietnam were working-class men, and a disproportionately high number of them were African Americans. Why?

The draft system had a number of loopholes young men could slip through, if they had enough privilege, social connections, or money.

One of the biggest draft loopholes were college deferments. Draft-age men were permitted to postpone their military service if they were college or graduate students. Young men whose families had enough money for college tuition could go to school to avoid the draft, whereas men from poorer families could not.

Talk is cheap. The war is not over until all the GI's are brought home alive.

CONNECT

A range of medical conditions could exempt a person from serving in Vietnam. Phil Ochs' song, "The Draft Dodgers' Rag," playfully describes some of these conditions. How many do you hear in this song? How is this song an act of protest?

🔍 Phil Ochs Dodgers

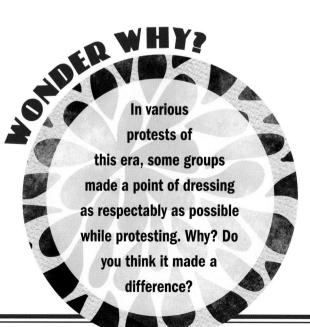

WONDER WHY?

In various protests of this era, some groups made a point of dressing as respectably as possible while protesting. Why? Do you think it made a difference?

Medical deferments were also a common way of avoiding duty. Men who suffered from a doctor-certified physical or mental ailment could be granted an exemption from military service. Thousands of young men rushed to doctors hoping to be diagnosed with an exemptible condition. Sometimes, sympathetic doctors exaggerated or even made up conditions for young men, particularly those they knew.

Because working class families might not have similar access to medical care or a personal relationship with a physician, they were less likely to receive medical exemptions.

The local draft board system also caused working-class men to be drafted in higher numbers. Draft boards were made up of men from the local community. These men had the power to decide who was fit to serve in the military and who should receive a deferment or exemption.

Families who had connections to draft board members often used those relationships—along with money—to pressure board members into excusing their draft-age children from service. Given that the overwhelming majority of board members were white, middle- and upper-class professionals, which families do you think were most likely to have those special connections and receive special treatment?

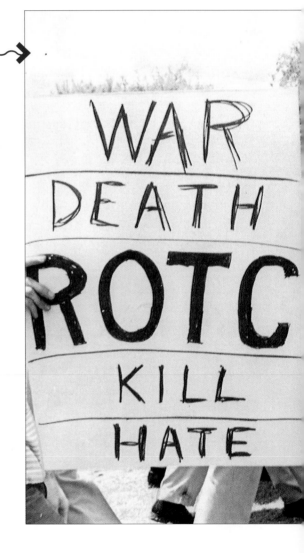

Vietnam War demonstration at Tulane University in New Orleans, Louisiana, 1969

Credit: Associated Press photo posted by manhhai (CC BY 2.0)

🦅 DRAFT CLASSIFICATION SYSTEM ᗏᗏ

The military and draft boards used the draft classification system to determine who was available to serve in the military. There were more than 25 classifications. Here are some of the most common types.

1-A: Fit for military service

1-O: Conscientious objector (CO), available for civilian work contributing to the national health, safety or interest. About 170,000 men were exempted from serving in the war because they were COs.

2-S: Student deferment

3-A: Deferred because military duty would cause hardship on family

4-G: Exempt because registrant is the sole surviving son of a family

4-F: Registrant not qualified for military service

CONNECT

Take a look as officials randomly select draft numbers for the year 1970. What do you notice about the people in the room? Why does it matter that no Black, Indigenous, or people of color are represented there?

🔍 **Thirteen draft lottery**

As inequities in the draft system became glaringly obvious, many protesters began to call for draft reform. They did this even as it put them at risk of losing their deferred status.

Beyond Draft Card Burning

Draft card burning wasn't the only kind of draft resistance. Some anti-war groups had draft counselors who would intercept draftees reporting for pre-induction to try to talk to them about possible deferments and exemptions.

Other young men turned in their draft cards instead of burning them. Draft resisters set up draft card turn-in locations in churches, school campuses, and, once, on the steps of the U.S. Department of Justice in Washington, DC. Some men sent their draft cards directly back to the military with a note explaining their anti-war position.

A march to the White House in October 1969, led by Coretta Scott King as part of the Moratorium to End the War in Vietnam

Most controversially, some 30,000 young men fled the United States to live in Canada and other countries to avoid fighting in the war. Because draft evasion was illegal, many of these men believed they were leaving their home, family, and friends for good.

The Price of Resistance

Draft resisters sometimes paid a high price for their protest. Many were ostracized by family, friends, and community members who believed they were disloyal and un-American for refusing to answer their country's call to fight. Hawks often harassed resisters during demonstrations, calling them traitors, commie-lovers, or cowards.

WONDER WHY?

What's the difference between a draft resister and draft evader (also called "draft dodger")? Some people would say nothing and others would say everything. What do you think the difference is, if any? Is there a moral distinction between the two?

Sometimes, protests turned violent. For example, on March 31, 1966, four draft resisters set fire to their draft cards on the Boston (Massachusetts) Courthouse steps before a crowd of 200 people. As they lit their cards, a mob of high school boys attacked, beating them severely. The resisters were charged with violating federal law and ultimately served time in prison. Most of the public and press supported the violent mob as "defenders of America."

Men who burned or turned in their draft cards also faced a special punishment—local draft boards immediately reclassified these resisters as A-1: "fit and ready for active military duty." But most draft resisters were prepared to go to jail anyway and refused to report for induction.

MUHAMMAD ALI

One of the most famous draft resisters was Muhammad Ali (1942–2016), the heavyweight boxing champion. He claimed CO status because killing was against his Muslim religion. He refused to be inducted and was stripped of his heavyweight title as punishment. The conviction was later overturned by the U.S. Supreme Court and his title was reinstated. Ali was a leader in the Black pride movement, which called for African Americans to embrace their culture and talents and avoid relying on white people for support. He dedicated a lot of time to caring for others and is remembered as a great humanitarian.

Protests Bring Draft Reform

By the late 1960s, Americans were exhausted by the war. The death toll of American soldiers and Vietnamese soldiers and civilians was growing ever higher, and the public was horrified by the ugly images of the war seen on television and in newspapers.

> "It is no longer a choice, my friends, between violence and nonviolence. It is either nonviolence or nonexistence."
>
> **Martin Luther King Jr.**
> speaking on the Vietnam War

Famous people, including Martin Luther King Jr., began to speak out against the war and the unfairness of the draft. The voice of dissenters became so powerful and the inequities of the draft so obvious that the government was forced to act.

As Richard Nixon (1913–1994) ran for president in 1968, he promised to end both the draft and U.S. involvement in the war. His goal was to make the Army entirely volunteer, which would neutralize the voices of draft resisters. After Nixon took office in January 1969, his administration changed the draft system to a lottery system. Draft-age men were randomly assigned numbers and had to report for induction if that number was called. Nixon also ended deferments for both graduate students and fathers.

Word Power!

What vocabulary words did you discover? Can you figure out the meanings of these words? Look in the glossary for help!

communist, conscientious objector, conscription, draft, neutralize, ostracize, pacifist, and privilege

But draft resistance continued even after these changes. Privileged people could still get deferments far more easily than those from the working class. Also, some people argued that the draft lottery wasn't producing truly random results.

Richard Nixon campaigning in 1968

The Draft Ends

In 1971, Nixon began acting on his promise to withdraw soldiers from Vietnam. He reduced monthly draft calls, sometimes canceling them altogether. After a year of secret negotiations, in October 1972, Nixon finally reached a peace agreement with North Vietnam. U.S. forces would leave Vietnam for good.

On January 27, 1973, the military announced the formal end of the draft. It was the first time since 1948 that no U.S. men would be drafted. The president's legal authority to draft troops expired in June 1973.

Since that time, the U.S. Congress has never sought to renew it or create another draft law.

While the Vietnam War draft resistance protests were highly divisive, they caused many Americans to pay closer attention to the war and think in a different way about the responsibilities of being an American citizen. In the end, these protests played a critical role in hastening the withdrawal of U.S. troops from Vietnam and the government's decision to end the draft altogether.

WONDER WHY?

During the war, about 570,000 men were classified as draft offenders, but charges were brought against only 210,000. Of those, 8,750 were convicted and 3,250 were jailed. Only 40 men were convicted of public draft card burning. Why do you think the government didn't bring more charges against draft resisters?

PROJECT

Hell No, We Won't Go!

Mottos and slogans are important parts of any protest. In the draft-resistance movement, iconic slogans included "Hell No, We Won't Go!" and "What if There was a War and Nobody Came?"

☮ **Let's consider the role mottos and slogans play in a protest.** Why are mottos and slogans important in protests?

☮ **Write down the different elements that make for a memorable motto or slogan.**

☮ **Think about an issue that you would like to protest or a message you would like to deliver to society.** Brainstorm two slogans that you would use if involved in a demonstration or march on this issue.

☮ **Pick one of the slogans and create a sign or poster that incorporates the slogan.**

· What would make the sign eye-catching or memorable?

· Does creating a sign for the slogan make you think differently about the elements needed for a good slogan? If so, why?

WONDER WHY?

Do you believe American citizens have a responsibility to speak out against the government if they believe the country is doing something immoral? How might this be good for the country?

TEXT TO WORLD

Do you think people would protest the draft if it were used as a tool today? Why or why not?

PROJECT

What's Free Speech?

The First Amendment to the U.S. Constitution forbids Congress from making a law that blocks the freedom of speech. But does burning a draft card count as speech? Draft resister David O'Brien believed it did and that the Draft Card Mutilation Act was unconstitutional because it tried to silence protesters. He took this argument all the way to the U.S. Supreme Court. But in 1968, the Court ruled that draft card burning was not protected speech and the law was constitutional. O'Brien served two years in prison for burning his card. Do some thinking and writing exercises to explore the issue of free speech.

☮ **What kind of speech do you think should be protected by the Constitution?** Should symbolic speech be protected? Should a lie be protected? What about hate speech? Write an essay explaining what you think free speech is—and isn't. Consider why and give examples.

☮ **Do you think draft card burning should constitute free speech?** Write an argument for or against draft card burning being free speech.

Read a summary of
O'Brien v. United States.

🔍 **MTSU O'Brien**

☮ **The U.S. Supreme Court ruled that the Constitution protected the Draft Card Mutilation Act because it helped the government to have a smoothly functioning draft system.** Do you agree? Why or why not?

☮ **Pretend you were eligible for the draft in the 1960s and you wanted to resist.** Can you think of any forms of symbolic speech that would have not violated the Draft Card Mutilation Act, yet would have attracted a lot of attention? Brainstorm a few ideas with a classmate.

Cesar Chavez at the Delano
UFW rally in Delano,
California, 1974.

THE DELANO GRAPE

STRIKE AND BOYCOTT

Do you ever think about how fruits and vegetables get to your table? It's thanks to the hard work of tens of thousands of farmworkers who pick each apple from a tree or dig each potato from the earth. During the 1960s, California farmworkers were paid meager wages and worked long hours under cruel conditions to ensure people had fresh fruit and vegetables in their kitchens—until workers came together to make a change.

49

American workers have long used strikes to fight for better pay and working conditions. But the Delano grape strike and boycott was historic because some of the most underprivileged persons in the country took on a powerful industry, fought for five long years, and won.

Grape harvest in Sacramento, California, 1938

Credit: Department of the Interior. Bureau of Indian Affairs. Sacramento Area Office. (1947)

Immigrant Migrant Workers

Since the United States's founding, wealthy landowners have relied on the poorest and least powerful members of society to harvest their crops. In the early seventeenth century, these workers were European indentured servants, followed by enslaved Africans.

1960s
For decades, the agricultural industry in California relies on migrant workers who are poorly paid and often mistreated.

1962
Cesar Chavez and Dolores Huerta organize the National Farmworkers' Association.

1965
Two large unions strike together and thousands of grape pickers refuse to work in Delano, California.

Children of migrant agricultural workers in San Joaquin Valley, California, 1940

Credit: Dorothea Lange, U.S. National Archives and Records Administration

IMMIGRATION AND REPATRIATION

Throughout history, the U.S. government has heartily welcomed and recruited immigrant laborers during times of need. However, as soon as white American workers felt that immigrants were lowering wages or taking jobs, there was a backlash, and these workers were often deported or banned outright.

CONNECT

To learn more, read about Mexican repatriation and the Chinese Exclusion Act of 1887 at these websites. Can you think of current examples of this kind of backlash?

 Washington deported 1 million

 PBS Chinese Exclusion Act

As the agricultural industry flourished in the nineteenth and twentieth centuries, hundreds of thousands of Mexicans, Chinese, and Japanese people immigrated to the United States to work the land.

1966
Chavez leads a 340-mile march from Delano to Sacramento, California, as part of the strike.

1968
Chavez goes on a hunger strike for 25 days. A grape boycott spreads across the country.

1970
Delano agricultural companies agree to raise wages and improve working conditions for workers.

By the 1960s, many farmworkers were foreign born or of foreign descent, especially in California. The vast majority were migrant workers, which meant that they traveled from town to town to plant, cultivate, or harvest, depending on the season. Some even migrated from Mexico to the United States for work, then returned home when the season ended.

Life was difficult for migrant farmworkers. Growers exploited them horribly and often treated them as if they weren't human. Workers labored under the blazing sun for up to 10 hours a day, yet their employers rarely provided them with access to toilets or even drinking water!

The job was also physically dangerous. Growers didn't care whether workers were present when spraying pesticides on the crops, so workers were often forced to inhale hazardous chemicals. Many also suffered from crippling back pain because of the hours they spent bending over in the fields picking or planting.

CONNECT

Watch a clip from the 1960 documentary, *Harvest of Shame*. It highlights the lives of African American farmworkers in Florida. The conditions were similar to those of immigrant laborers. Is there anything that surprises you about the conditions of the laborers or the reactions of some of the people being interviewed?

🔍 **CBS Harvest of Shame**

THE BRACERO PROGRAM

During World War II, the United States and Mexico created the Emergency Labor Program, better known as the "bracero" program (*brazos* means "arms" in Spanish). This program allowed U.S. farms to hire Mexicans workers on a short-term contract. After the war ended, landowners were still permitted to employ braceros, but many hired them without a contract, which was illegal. This way, they could pay them very low wages, avoid paying for health care, and have them deported if they complained. Hiring braceros illegally was unfair to both braceros and U.S. farmworkers. The government ended the program in 1964.

Many workers lived in camps on the growers' properties during harvest season. These camps were often dirty, overcrowded, and lacked running water. Germs and sickness spread easily. Growers deducted housing costs from the pay of workers who lived in these camps.

To make matters worse, migrant farmworkers were severely underpaid. Many earned about 90 cents per hour, which was much less than the 1965 minimum wage of $1.25.

Even paying this low rate, some dishonest growers would find excuses to underpay their workers or not pay them at all.

Farmworkers were unhappy with their situations, but didn't know how to improve them. Growers seemed to hold all the power. Unlike workers in other industries, farmworkers didn't have a strong union to protect their rights—that is, until the Civil Rights Era.

WONDER WHY?

Because the pay was so low, many migrant families needed their children to work in the fields to keep food on the table. Although the United States had strict child labor laws, the authorities looked the other way. Why might that be?

Mexicans working in a flax field in Oregon, 1946

Mexican workers await legal employment in the United States as part of the bracero program, 1954

Credit: Los Angeles Times (Firm), Publisher, PD

In May 1965, AWOC grape pickers held a strike of vineyards in Coachella Valley, California. They demanded a 15-cent pay raise and contracts promising improved working conditions and benefits. The strike lasted a week. The growers gave the workers a raise, but refused to offer contracts.

In 1959, farmworkers in Stockton, California, formed the Agricultural Workers Organizing Committee (AWOC). Led by a determined man named Larry Itliong (1913–1977), this union was mostly composed of Filipino men. Itliong had already spent decades organizing to protect farmworkers' rights, and he was unafraid to speak out. Under Itliong's leadership, the union grew to thousands of members.

Months after the Coachella Valley strike, AWOC members migrated to Delano, California, to harvest table grapes. Delano growers offered very low wages and refused to negotiate. The AWOC was prepared to strike again. But this time, they decided to hold out for contracts. They knew that without a contract, they'd run into the same problem every year.

WHAT IS A UNION?

A union is a group of workers from the same industry who come together to protect their rights and interests. They bargain collectively for fair wages and better working conditions or they raise grievances. Unions are meant to redistribute the balance of power between employees and employers.

Historically, employers have discouraged employees from forming or joining unions. They fear having to spend more time and money meeting union requirements. Even some employees have objected to having to join unions at their jobs—they don't want to pay the mandatory fees or follow guidelines set by the group.

This strike promised to be a big one, and the AWOC needed all the help it could get. Itliong contacted Cesar Chavez (1927–1993), the leader of a newly formed Chicano farmworkers union. From there, history was made.

Enter Cesar Chavez

Cesar Chavez was a soft-spoken community activist in Delano who had grown up in a migrant, farmworking family. Despite his gentle nature, he was fiercely committed to helping Chicanos stand up for themselves. As director for the Community Service Organization, he helped register Chicanos to vote, educated them about their rights, set up citizenship classes for them, and more.

Cesar Chavez, 1974
Credit: Joel Levine (CC BY 3.0)

THE MANONGS

The Manongs were the hundreds of thousands of Filipino migrant farmworkers who immigrated to the United States during the 1930s and 1940s. While most Asians were barred from immigrating because of the Chinese Exclusion Act of 1887, Filipinos were allowed because the Philippines was a U.S. territory. The Manongs (a term meaning "older brother") played a critical role in the fight for farmworkers' rights.

CONNECT

Learn more about this often-overlooked people in this article. Why were these workers used as a scapegoat during times of economic uncertainty?

🔍 **NPCA Manongs worker movement**

But he was especially determined to help farmworkers. In 1962, he formed the National Farmworkers' Association (NFWA) union with Dolores Huerta (1930–), a Chicana community organizer. They hoped that with enough union members, they could pressure landowners to treat workers more fairly.

"Chicano" is a term for Americans of Mexican descent.

It was hard to convince farmworkers to join the union. When farmworkers had tried to organize unions in the past, the growers had threatened, fired, or beaten them—or had them deported. With time, however, Chavez and Huerta were able to persuade more and more workers to join.

By 1965, the NFWA had more than 1,000 members. Chavez and Huerta were pleased, but they wanted to grow even stronger before they undertook a major action. When Itliong contacted them about the strike in Delano, they had to make a decision fast. Itliong warned that AWOC would be striking with or without them, but they'd have a better chance of success if the two unions acted together.

Chavez presented the proposition to union members, and they enthusiastically voted in favor of joining the strike.

¡Huelga!

On September 20, 1965, NFWA members joined the strike. Instead of working, they picketed on the road near the vineyards. They repeatedly shouted, "¡Huelga!" (Strike!) as they picketed and encouraged non-union workers who weren't striking to join them. With both unions striking, thousands of grape pickers had abandoned the fields.

The National Labor Relations Act of 1935 prevents employers from firing or threatening employees for creating or joining a union. But farmworkers were explicitly excluded from this law.

The growers were furious. The loss of workers meant the grapes were at risk of rotting on the vine. They quickly brought in other grape pickers, but the growers still wanted to stop the strike.

DOLORES HUERTA

We hear much more about Cesar Chavez than we do Dolores Huerta, but she was equally indispensable to the farmworker's cause. Huerta worked behind the scenes, lobbying politicians to create more favorable laws for farmworkers. Thanks to her efforts, California lawmakers passed regulations allowing farmworkers to receive disability and unemployment insurance, among other things. Huerta was also responsible for negotiating farmworker contracts with the growers, the first woman to do so.

Dolores Huerta in 2013
Credit: U.S. Department of Labor

Part of a mural by Melchor Ramirez honoring Cesar Chavez in Tucson, Arizona

Credit: Carol Highsmith, photographer

Growers tried several tactics to intimidate the strikers and lessen their influence, including playing loud music to drown out the shouts of "¡Huelga!," turning vicious dogs on them, and using crop dusters to spray them with pesticides. Others fired shots above the strikers' heads or hired people to threaten and beat them.

The strikers didn't fight back. Chavez greatly admired Mahatma Gandhi (1869–1948), a nonviolent Indian resistance leader, and Martin Luther King Jr. and believed in the power of nonviolent protest. He had made union members pledge never to use aggression against growers, even if beaten.

Months passed. Chavez and Huerta traveled all around California to drum up support for the strike. They spoke at universities, churches, and with politicians, describing appalling wages and working conditions for farmworkers. They outlined the unions' demands and emphasized that the issues weren't just about work, but were also a question of dignity and civil rights. Why was this significant?

WONDER WHY?

Cesar Chavez often referred to the union as "*El Movimiento*" (The Movement) or "*La Causa*" (The Cause). Why do you think he characterized it that way?

Many people were sympathetic. Thousands, including unions in other industries, donated money or food toward the cause. Students, many already active in the civil rights and anti-war movements, were eager to help. They spoke out about the problem, and some even joined the picket lines.

WONDER WHY?

Why did most civil rights leaders insist on keeping the protests nonviolent even if people abused the protestors? Name three reasons.

In March 1966, Chavez led a 340-mile march of 75 farmworkers from Delano to Sacramento, the capital of California. People cheered the workers as they passed through towns and hundreds of supporters joined them. When they reached the capital 25 days later, a crowd of 8,000 people greeted them.

New Tactics

When the grape harvest season ended, Chavez and Huerta wanted to keep pressure on the growers and hold the public's attention. They called for a boycott of non-union-approved grapes. They also organized union members to use picket lines to block delivery trucks carrying the growers' grapes. Sometimes, supportive truck drivers refused to unload the grapes. This tactic resulted in embarrassing delivery delays for the growers and brought more publicity to the cause.

These strategies brought some success. After the union called for the boycott of one large company that owned both grape fields and other products, the company gave in. It gave strikers raises and contracts that promised regular work, improved working conditions, and health benefits. But there was still work to be done so that all companies would grant farmworkers these rights.

SURVIVING THE STRIKE

How did people who were already poor live while on strike, when no money was coming in? Some strikers picked crops for non-grape growers or took on other jobs. The union also gave financial support to strikers through union dues and public donations. Most importantly, the Chicano and Filipino communities looked out for one another and donated food, clothes, and money to families in need.

Keeping the Peace

The strike continued for one year, then two. In the third year, some strikers were getting impatient. They found it difficult to withstand the violent treatment by growers without retaliating. Some people wanted to fight back.

Chavez was dismayed. He decided to stop eating until union members agreed to remain peaceful. He began his fast at the Delano union headquarters in February 1968. For 25 days, he ate no food and drank only water. Hundreds of people came to visit him as he fasted, including U.S. Senator Robert Kennedy (1925–1968). The public sent donations and farmworkers prayed for him daily. When he ended the fast, all talk of using violence stopped.

In August 1966, the AWOC and NFWA joined to form one large union called the United Farm Workers Organizing Committee (UFW). Chavez was named president. The union exists to this day.

A sculpture of Chavez in Sacramento, California

Credit: The Jon B. Lovelace Collection of California Photographs in Carol M. Highsmith's America Project, Library of Congress, Prints and Photographs Division

Boycott Grapes

After the fast, Chavez decided to call for a boycott of *all* California grapes. He even asked people to boycott supermarkets that sold California grapes.

By now, Chavez and the movement were well known to many Americans. Countless people were moved by the farmworkers' struggle and determination and were eager to boycott grapes. Across the country, volunteers picketed stores selling California grapes. Many Chicano and Chicana students led boycotts on their school campuses. Hundreds of strikers traveled around the country to tell their stories.

Victory!

The boycott was a huge success. Millions of people around the country stopped eating California grapes. Even schoolchildren knew that by boycotting grapes, they were helping poor farmworkers.

Chicago, 1973

Credit: Paul Sequeira, photographer

WONDER WHY?

What are some of the reasons that Chavez might have chosen fasting as a means of protest?

" Every moment is an organizing opportunity, every person a potential activist, every minute a chance to change the world."

Dolores Huerta

Cesar Chavez, 1979

Credit: *U.S. News & World Report* magazine collection (Library of Congress)

By 1970, the grape growers had lost millions of dollars from the boycott. They had to admit defeat. They raised farmworker wages by as much as 60 percent and signed contracts with the union guaranteeing better working conditions, health benefits, and other protections.

Chavez and Huerta continued advocating for farmworkers' rights for decades afterward.

"However important the struggle is and however much misery, poverty, and exploitation exist, we know that it cannot be more important than one human life."

Cesar Chavez

Thanks to their efforts, in 1975, the California legislature passed the California Agricultural Labor Relations Act, which gave collective bargaining power to state farmworkers.

Farmworkers today still struggle to obtain living wages and contracts from powerful landowners. But, thanks to Chavez and Huerta, they have unions and laws in place to help them. Even better—they know that nothing is impossible.

Word Power!

What vocabulary words did you discover? Can you figure out the meanings of these words? Look in the glossary for help!

backlash, exploit, intimidate, migrant, picket, strike, and union

THE WORK OF A BOYCOTT

It's hard to imagine the amount of effort that went into such a large boycott. Huerta led the boycott in New York City. She had to identify how the grapes arrived in the city and where they were being distributed, rally supporters, and organize the picket lines. She also spoke with numerous politicians, colleges, priests, newspapers, and television and radio stations to seek support. And that was just in *one* city!

ROBERT F. KENNEDY

The grape strike attracted the attention of many politicians, especially U.S. Senator Robert F. Kennedy. Kennedy came to Delano to discuss the situation and became a firm champion of the cause. He became friends with Huerta and worked closely with her to resolve the farmworkers' plight until he was assassinated in 1968.

Robert Kennedy, 1963
Credit: *U.S. News & World Report* magazine collection

PROJECT

Blueprint a Boycott

Did you know that there are many calls for boycotts right now? Certain groups seek the boycotts of chocolate, Amazon.com, and even the National Football League. What are these boycotts about? Let's find out.

☮ **Identify five boycotts currently underway.** Create a chart for these boycotts and answer the following questions for each example.

· Who is calling for the boycott?

· Why are they calling for the boycott?

· Who are the leaders of the boycott?

· How is the boycott being publicized?

· Do you think the boycott will be successful? Why or why not?

☮ **Pretend you're in charge of organizing one boycott on your list.** How would you go about it? Write a strategy for the boycott. As you plan, consider the following factors.

· What is the "story" that will make the public sympathetic to the boycott?

· What is the ultimate goal of the boycott?

· What obstacles will you have to overcome to achieve success?

· How would you try to overcome these obstacles?

· How would you bring the boycott to national attention?

· Which allies might be interested in supporting the boycott? How would you recruit them?

TEXT TO WORLD

Is the food you eat grown, harvested, and transported ethically? How can you find out?

Design a Protest Flag

What significance do flags have in protest movements? Chavez had a union flag created right from the start. It had a black Aztec eagle in a white circle with a red background. The color black represented the dark situation of the farmworker. The white circle expressed hope. Red reflected the sacrifice and hard work that union members would need. The Aztec eagle represented the Mexican-American heritage of most union members.

⚛ **Think about an issue you feel strongly about.** What kind of flag would you create to rally people behind your cause?

⚛ **Brainstorm themes you want the flag to represent.** Are you trying to convey dignity? Strength? Love? Determination? Pride?

⚛ **Consider how to convey the message.** What kind of symbols or shapes would you include? What colors would you use and why? How might numbers figure into the design? Might you include a written message?

⚛ **Sketch your design.** Use colored paper or pencils. If you have trouble drawing certain shapes freehand, consider using stamps or stencils. Don't forget to think about how the back of the flag should look.

CONNECT

Need inspiration? Watch this video explaining the basics of flag design.

🔍 **YouTube How to Actually Design a Flag**

CHAPTER FOUR

THE STONEWALL
RIOTS

Most protestors during the Civil Rights Era tried to practice nonviolent protest. But when faced with endless unfair treatment, almost anyone can be pushed to their limits. The LGBTQ liberation movement arose out of such a moment—an overwhelming feeling of having had enough.

FAST FACTS

WHAT?
The Stonewall riots in New York City

WHY?
To show pride in being LGBTQ and to gain acceptance in society

WHEN?
June 28–July 3, 1969

HOW?
At yet another crackdown by law enforcement on LGBTQ people at the Stonewall Inn in 1969, the crowd fought back, sparking a series of marches and parades that let people show their pride in ways that had always been prohibited.

Throughout most of U.S. history, gays, lesbians, bisexuals, and transgender people could not openly embrace their sexual or gender identities without putting their lives, jobs, and personal relationships at great risk. American society thought of homosexuality as abnormal, and the medical community classified it as a mental illness.

Legal discrimination was everywhere. Laws forbid LGBTQ people to love each other, marry, serve in the military, or hold state or federal government positions. If an employer found out an employee was gay or transgender, the employee could be fired immediately. Gay characters in film or television were forbidden. In society, LGBTQ people often faced exclusion, mockery, or violence.

Unsurprisingly, most LGBTQ people were afraid to reveal their sexual orientation or gender identity openly. But, if people knew where to look, they could find secret spaces where they could be themselves for a little while.

SOCIETY FOR HUMAN RIGHTS

The Society for Human Rights was the first-known gay rights organization in the United States. Founded in 1924 by a German immigrant named Henry Gerber (1892–1972), the society was forced to disband after only one year when the police raided it. Nonetheless, Gerber continued to write in support of legitimizing homosexuality. Gerber's house in Chicago, Illinois, is a historic landmark, thanks to his contributions to the LGBTQ community.

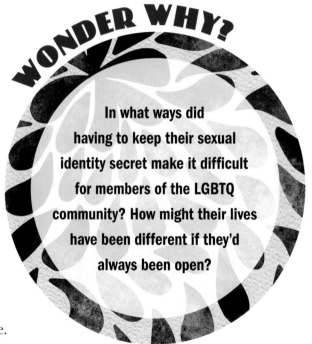

WONDER WHY?

In what ways did having to keep their sexual identity secret make it difficult for members of the LGBTQ community? How might their lives have been different if they'd always been open?

CIVIL RIGHTS TIMELINE

1960s
Members of the LGBTQ community suffer decades of mistreatment and denial, prevented by law from being open in public.

1966
Customers at Gene Compton's Cafeteria in San Francisco, California, riot after being harassed by the police.

1969
Police raid the Stonewall Inn, a Mafia-run bar where LGBTQ people were able to dance and socialize with members of the same sex.

Each July 4th, from 1965 through 1969, citizens gathered in front of Independence Hall in Philadelphia, Pennsylvania, to protest the discrimination gay and lesbian individuals faced throughout the United States.

Credit: NPS PHOTO

Safe Spaces

In the mid-twentieth century, numerous bars and clubs in major cities across the country catered to LGBTQ clientele. Gay bars were safe spaces for the community, except when the outside world came barging in. The police regularly raided gay bars and arrested LGBTQ patrons for violating various laws, such as "impersonating" a woman, dancing with someone of the same gender, or holding hands.

THREE-ARTICLE RULE

The police often used nineteenth-century anti-crossdressing laws to criminalize homosexuality and transgender people. Unofficially, the police sometimes used what the LGBTQ community called the "three-article rule." Under this rule, LGBTQ people reportedly had to show police that they were wearing three pieces of "gender-appropriate clothing" to avoid arrest.

1969
Riots continue for days after the initial one at the Stonewall Inn.

1970
The first Gay Pride Parade is held in New York City to commemorate the Stonewall Inn riots, ushering in an era of revived protest for LGBTQ rights.

2015
The U.S. Supreme Court rules that state laws banning same-sex marriage are unconstitutional.

Police officers also often entered bars pretending to be gay and then arrested bar patrons if someone expressed interest in them. So, although LGBTQ people could relax and be themselves in these places, they were never entirely free of the fear that the police could disrupt their fun or arrest and humiliate them at any time.

New York City was home to many gay bars, but not all bars were the same. Some catered to gay members who kept a low profile and dressed in conventional clothes. Some bars were for the wealthy or well-educated set. But there was one bar that stood out because it welcomed all in the LGBTQ community, from transgender people to runaway gay teens.

The Stonewall Inn

The Stonewall Inn was a rundown, two-room bar in the Manhattan neighborhood of Greenwich Village.

In New York City, it was even illegal for businesses to serve alcohol to gay people.

WONDER WHY?

Why do you think that the ability to dance together was a big deal, so important that the LGBTQ community would risk arrest?

It was popular not just because all were welcome, but also because it was one of the few places in the city where the LGBTQ community could dance with one another, which was illegal under New York law.

Legalities didn't concern the owners of the Stonewall Inn. It was run by the Mafia, an organized crime syndicate. The Mafia owned gay bars all around the city, serving overpriced alcoholic drinks to the clientele.

The Mafia also blackmailed wealthier guests by threatening to publicize their sexuality if they didn't pay up.

Even though the Mafia owned Stonewall, the police still raided it. But corrupt police officers accepted money from the Mafia to give bar owners a warning first. In turn, the owners warned customers of raids, changing the color of the lights on the dance floor so they would know to stop dancing.

During typical raids, the police would burst into the place and announce the raid, confiscate the alcohol, and then send people dressed as women into another room to have their genders determined by female officers. The police would take everyone's name, release the people who hadn't violated any laws, and arrest the people who had.

But when police raided the Stonewall Inn in the wee hours of June 28, 1969, nothing went as anyone expected.

Enough is Enough!

On the night of the fateful raid, more than 200 people were dancing and having fun inside the Stonewall Inn. But among them were four undercover police officers, making notes on employees and the bar patrons to be able to identify them as law breakers.

CONNECT

Read an article about the Stonewall riots at this website. What characteristics did the people who fought for LGBTQ rights have in common with people who protested for labor rights and equality for African Americans?

🔍 Guardian Stonewall anniversary

DRESSED IN DRAG

Drag shows are performances where the performers are wearing clothes more often worn by a different gender. They might sing, dance, perform skits, or do comedy. In the past, drag performers were often arrested going to or from shows, which was not only inconvenient, it affected their ability to earn a living. A drag performer was not necessarily gay or transgender. Why do you think law enforcement and others felt threatened enough to make arrests?

Around 1:20 a.m., six police officers burst into the bar and announced the raid. But as they began the usual separation process, something unusual happened—many customers refused to cooperate. Gender nonconforming people resisted going with the officers to have their genders verified and men refused to show their IDs.

The police began to release customers one by one. But instead of leaving the area, drag performers stood outside the bar and began to tease and mock the police by primping their hair, blowing kisses, or doing other gender nonconforming acts. Passersby stopped and cheered. How might these actions be considered a form of protest?

The police, unused to resistance from the gay community and seeing that they were outnumbered, called for backup. A patrol wagon arrived, and the police took three drag performers outside. The crowd began to boo the police.

Next, the police brought out a handcuffed lesbian and tried to put her in a patrol car. After an officer treated her roughly, she yelled for the crowd to "do something!" Someone threw a brick at the police. Other people began to throw pennies, dimes, and bottles. The riot had begun.

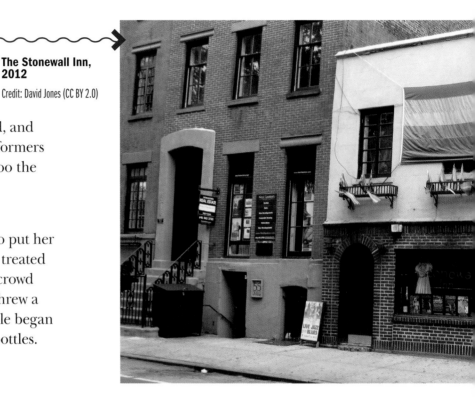

The Stonewall Inn, 2012

Credit: David Jones (CC BY 2.0)

Riot Ensues

As the rioting intensified, the police inspector leading the raid decided to barricade his team inside the bar, along with several transgender women, until more backup arrived.

The crowd used a parking meter as a battering ram to bash open the bar's door. People began throwing more coins, beer bottles, and stones.

THE COMPTON'S CAFETERIA RIOT

The Stonewall riots weren't the first time the LGBTQ community stood up to police officers. In 1966, transgender women and gay drag performers in San Francisco, California, rioted at a local diner called Gene Compton's Cafeteria. The riot began when a police officer grabbed a transgender woman while preparing to arrest her. She threw coffee in the officer's face in response. After that, the crowd erupted and fought the police. "We were tired of being arrested for nothing, arrested for being who we wanted to be," explained Felicia Flames (1946–), a self-described transsexual woman who often went to Compton's Cafeteria during the 1960s.

GENE COMPTON'S CAFETERIA RIOT 1966

HERE MARKS THE SITE OF GENE COMPTON'S CAFETERIA WHERE A RIOT TOOK PLACE ONE AUGUST NIGHT WHEN TRANSGENDER WOMEN AND GAY MEN STOOD UP FOR THEIR RIGHTS AND FOUGHT AGAINST POLICE BRUTALITY, POVERTY, OPPRESSION AND DISCRIMINATION IN THE TENDERLOIN.
WE, THE TRANSGENDER, GAY, LESBIAN AND BISEXUAL COMMUNITY, ARE DEDICATING THIS PLAQUE TO THESE HEROES OF OUR CIVIL RIGHTS MOVEMENT.

DEDICATED JUNE 22, 2006

🐾 MARSHA P. JOHNSON & SYLVIA RIVERA 🕊

Who threw the first brick? LGBTQ lore says that it was Marsha P. Johnson (1945–1992), an African American transgender woman, but there's no record of it and Johnson herself has said in interviews that it wasn't her. But there's no question that she, Sylvia Rivera (1951–2002), and other transgender women played an instrumental role in the uprising that night. After Stonewall, Johnson and Rivera became well-known transgender activists, creating an organization known as STAR (Street Transvestite Action Revolutionaries). Through STAR, they gave shelter and support to countless transgender and nonbinary youth in New York City. The city is currently planning to erect a statue honoring Johnson and Rivera in Greenwich Village.

Some even hurled homemade firebombs at the building and slashed the tires of police cars. Fistfights broke out between the police and transgender women and drag performers. The crowd hurled insults at the police and shouted, "Gay power" and "We want freedom!"

"We all had a collective feeling like we'd had enough. . . . It wasn't anything tangible anybody said to anyone else, it was just kind of like everything over the years had come to a head on that one particular night in that one particular place. Everyone in the crowd felt that we were never going to go back. It was time to reclaim something that had always been taken from us. . . ."

Michael Fader, Stonewall rioter

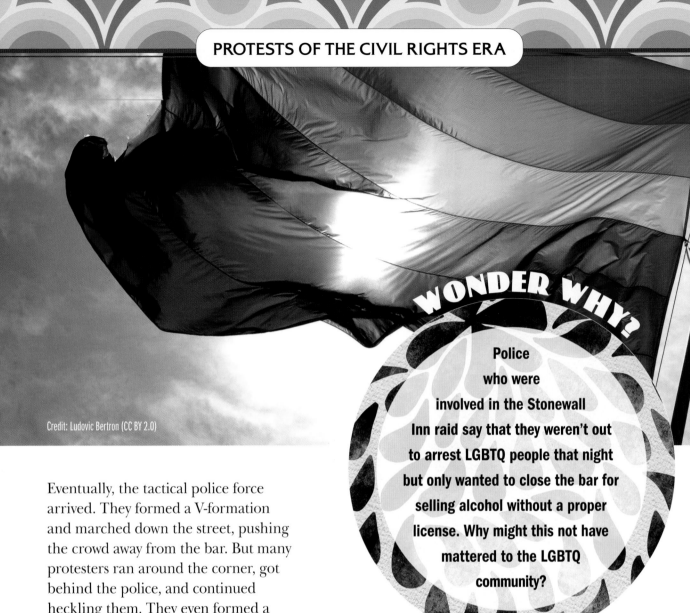

Credit: Ludovic Bertron (CC BY 2.0)

WONDER WHY?

Police who were involved in the Stonewall Inn raid say that they weren't out to arrest LGBTQ people that night but only wanted to close the bar for selling alcohol without a proper license. Why might this not have mattered to the LGBTQ community?

Eventually, the tactical police force arrived. They formed a V-formation and marched down the street, pushing the crowd away from the bar. But many protesters ran around the corner, got behind the police, and continued heckling them. They even formed a can-can dance line and kicked their legs at the officers like dancers, singing:

We are the Village girls
We wear our hair in curls
We wear our dungarees
Above our nelly knees.

The police finally got control of the area around 4 a.m. and cleared the area. But the LGBTQ community was just getting started.

Pride Grows

On the night following the riot, hundreds of LGBTQ people and supporters gathered at Stonewall again, spilling into the adjoining streets. Although the bar was half destroyed, people wanted to be near the place where the community had fought back.

Newly empowered, many people felt free to celebrate their identities out in the open. Some scrawled graffiti reading "Gay Power" and "Legalize gay bars" on the bar's exterior walls. By nightfall, the crowd was so immense that the police arrived again. Once again, the LGBTQ community stood up to them. This pattern would continue for the next five days.

Even as people joyfully gathered at Stonewall, LGBTQ groups were making plans to transform this newfound empowerment into a full-blown civil rights movement. But the community was divided on how to go about it. Some groups wanted to ease slowly into change, but others, inspired by the Civil Rights and Black Power Movements, wanted bigger and bolder action.

Craig Rodwell Takes Action

Gay activist Craig Rodwell (1940–1993) was an enthusiastic participant in the Stonewall Inn riots on the first night. Afterward, he knew that the time had come for the LGBTQ community to fight even harder for its rights. The next night, he returned to Stonewall and passed out leaflets, calling for both the Mafia and the police to stay out of gay bars and for gay business owners to take charge instead.

A gay pride parade in 1976, New York City

Credit: Warren K. Leffler, photographer, *U.S. News & World Report* magazine collection

Rodwell was no stranger to pushing for change. He was vice-president of the New York chapter of the Mattachine Society, a gay rights organization founded in the 1950s. This organization took a restrained approach to activism. But Rodwell, owner of a gay bookshop, had long wanted the organization to be more militant.

Five months after Stonewall, Rodwell and fellow activists Fred Sargeant (1948–), Ellen Broidy (unknown), and Linda Rhodes (unknown) came up with the idea to hold an annual march on the last Sunday in June to commemorate the Stonewall riots. The march would have no age restrictions or dress code—people could simply come as they were.

The planning took months and was sometimes problematic—more than a dozen LGBTQ rights groups were involved. Brenda Howard (1946–2005), a bisexual LGBTQ activist, handled so much of the organization that to this day, she is known as the "Mother of Pride."

MATTACHINE SOCIETY'S ANNUAL REMINDER

From 1965 through 1969, members of the Mattachine Society and the sister lesbian organization, Daughters of Bilitis, held a silent protest every July 4 in front of Independence Hall in Philadelphia, Pennsylvania. The protest was intended to be an annual reminder that gays and lesbians still did not have equal rights in society. Participants were required to wear gender-conforming clothes—men in suits and women in skirts or dresses. Organizers felt it was important to show society that gays and lesbians aligned with mainstream values. The last annual reminder took place a few days after Stonewall. Many people felt it was too outdated. Why might people have felt that way?

LGBTQ Pride Goes on Parade

On June 28, 1970, for the first time, thousands of members of the LGBTQ community gathered together in New York City to openly show pride in their identity. The march started with a thousand or so people but swelled as an increasing number of LGBTQ bystanders gathered the courage to join in.

This first march was officially known as the Christopher Street Liberation Day in honor of the street where the Stonewall Inn was situated. Later, it became known as the LGBTQ Pride Parade.

The transgender pride flag

CONNECT

Watch a couple of interviews with people who were present at the Stonewall Riots. How have things changed between now and then? Can you think of any group today that faces issues similar to those faced by LGBTQ people back then?

 Euronews LGBT pride

The bisexual pride flag

The current version of the gay pride flag, which has taken different forms in the past

A rally for National Coming Out Day on October 10, 2011
Credit: AUSTEN HUFFORD/Daily (CC BY 2.0)

The atmosphere was jubilant. People carried signs and banners with messages such as "Gay Pride!" and "Gay is Good!" The crowd proceeded from Greenwich Village to Shepard's Meadow in Central Park, a span of 51 blocks. In the park, participants held what organizers called a "gay-in," where people danced together, laughed, and reveled in simply being who they were.

WONDER WHY?

The march organizers thought about using "Gay Power" as the theme of the march, but very deliberately decided to use "Gay Pride" instead. Why do you think they made this choice?

Other cities also held gay pride marches during the same period, including San Francisco and Los Angeles in California, and Chicago, Illinois. The following year, even more cities joined in. Today, hundreds of cities across the United States and around the world remember Stonewall and the beginnings of LGBTQ equality by holding pride marches and other events in June.

Word Power!

What vocabulary words did you discover? Can you figure out the meanings of these words? Look in the glossary for help!

confiscate, empower, gender identity, homosexuality, invisibility, and transgender

A New Day Dawns

Since Stonewall, the LGBTQ community has made tremendous strides toward acceptance. Four years after the riot, the American Psychiatric Association eliminated homosexuality as a mental disorder.

CONNECT

A Gallup poll shows that in 2019, 93 percent of people questioned think gays and lesbians should have equal rights to job opportunities, compared to 53 percent in 1977. Take a look at the poll at this website. What other changes do you note? Is there anything surprising about these statistics?

 gallup gay lesbian rights

Gay rights and ally organizations fought against numerous discriminatory state and federal laws in the courts and got them struck down. Most notably, in 2015, the U.S. Supreme Court ruled that state laws banning same-sex marriage were unconstitutional. LGBTQ citizens finally have the right to marry who they love!

The LGBTQ community is still struggling to gain social acceptance and equal rights, but the Stonewall riot was a turning point. From that time onward, the community refused to remain in the shadows of society or accept being treated as second-class citizens.

The month of June is now celebrated as LGBTQ+ Pride Month across the United States.

PROJECT

Fighting Invisibility

The LGBTQ community has fought many things to find societal acceptance, including discrimination, prejudice, ignorance, and harassment. But before they could address any of these obstacles on a wide scale, they had to fight something else: invisibility. Let's consider what invisibility means and how to avoid it.

☮ **According to Wikipedia, social invisibility "refers to a group of people in society who have been separated or systematically ignored by the majority of the public."** Consider these questions.

· What are the disadvantages of being invisible to society?

· What disadvantages does invisibility bring to a group? For individuals in that group?

· How can bringing visibility to a group help that group? How can it help society?

☮ **Since Stonewall, how has the LGBTQ community fought against invisibility?** Among other things, consider symbols, colors, and mottos the community has embraced.

☮ **Brainstorm other groups of people who may feel invisible to society.** Do you think they're justified in feeling invisible? Why?

☮ **Chose one "invisible" group.** Write a paragraph describing how group members might make themselves and their issues more visible.

☮ **Write a short story about a person who is an "invisible" member of society who decides to take a bold step to bring visibility to their group.**

TEXT TO WORLD
Have you ever repeatedly felt invisible in a situation? What were the circumstances? How did it make you feel? What effects did it have on your life? What did you do about the situation?

Humor in Protest

The Stonewall riot was a serious event, but it also had certain humorous elements, such as the protest kick line and the playful chants. What positive role can humor play in protest? How might humor in a protest backfire?

- ☮ **Do some research on funny moments during different types of protests.**

  · Do certain kinds of protest lend themselves better to humor?

  · Why or why not?

  · Does timing have anything to do with why a population might find something funny?

- ☮ **Choose a social or political issue.** Design a humorous sign, banner, or slogan, or create a funny performative protest, song, or chant to bring attention to a particular issue. As you create, consider these questions.

  · Who will find the message funny?

  · What makes the message funny?

  · How does it communicate a more serious message?

CONNECT

Listen to interviews with activists, including organizer Ellen Broidy, from the first LGBTQ Pride Parade. How does listening to firsthand accounts change your perspective of an event?

🔎 **Broidy Stonewall Oral History Project**

" A riot is the language of the unheard."

Martin Luther King Jr.

WOMEN'S EQUALITY DAY

UNITE FOR WOMANS EMANCIPATION

Women's March for Equality August 26th, 1970

Designed by Peter Hemmer for the Defense Equal Opportunity Management Institute

A poster for the 2012 Women's Equality Day celebration

CHAPTER FIVE

WOMEN'S STRIKE FOR

EQUALITY

FASTFACTS

WHAT?
Women's Strike for Equality

WHY?
To fight for equal treatment for women

WHEN?
August 26, 1970

HOW?
As women grew more aware of their own mistreatment, they organized events to draw attention to sexual discrimination and harassment and worked to demand equal rights.

We're so used to seeing women in almost every role in society these days that it's easy to forget that, before the 1960s, women were constantly–and legally–discriminated against. That we may forget is thanks to the women of the Civil Rights Era who demanded rights equal to men.

The Women's Strike for Equality was a nationwide event in which an estimated 150,000 women participated—the largest women's demonstration since the early twentieth century. The demonstration showed the power of women when unified and made women's concerns a serious part of the national conversation.

A Woman's Place

Throughout most of U.S. history, American society expected women and men to follow established gender roles. Women were to get married, stay at home, and take care of domestic matters, such as cooking and childrearing. Men were to earn money to support the family.

World War II changed things. During the 1940s, millions of men went off to fight, leaving businesses with a severely diminished workforce. Women stepped in, capably taking over traditionally male jobs, such as truck driving and welding.

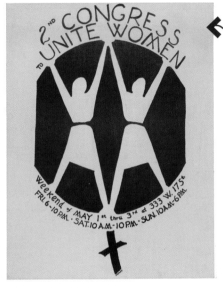

Poster for the 1970 Second Congress to Unite Women, organized by NOW. Lesbians protested this meeting, calling themselves the Lavender Menace.

"Simply put, feminism is a movement to end sexism, sexist exploitation, and oppression. . . . As all advocates of feminist politics know, most people do not understand sexism, or if they do, they think it is not a problem."

bell hooks (1952–), African American author, professor, and activist

CIVIL RIGHTS TIMELINE

1940s
When men go to fight in World War II, women take over their jobs outside the home. When the war ends, many women are fired and encouraged to return to homemaking.

1963
Betty Friedan publishes *The Feminine Mystique* after interviewing many white, middle-class women about their lives.

1963
The U.S. Congress passes the Equal Pay Act to ensure equal pay for equal work, regardless of gender.

When the war ended, most women were fired from their jobs and encouraged to go back to homemaking. What's more, society made clear that staying home was their patriotic duty. How do you think women felt about that?

"Top Women" at U.S. Steel's Gary, Indiana, Works, 1940–1945

A Woman's Duty

During the 1950s, the United States entered a Cold War with the former Soviet Union, a communist country. The U.S. government feared that if communism spread, it would take root in America and destroy what was called the "American way of life."

For women, the American way of life meant being a traditional housewife. A woman was expected to keep a comfortable home, raise happy children, look as attractive as possible, and support her husband without considering herself. By playing this role, she was supposedly helping to show that life in the United States was better than in the Soviet Union.

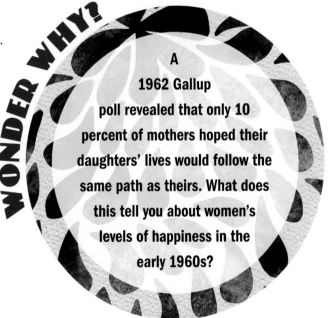

WONDER WHY?

A 1962 Gallup poll revealed that only 10 percent of mothers hoped their daughters' lives would follow the same path as theirs. What does this tell you about women's levels of happiness in the early 1960s?

1964
Title VII of the Civil Rights Act of 1964 is enacted, prohibiting sex discrimination.

1966
The National Organization of Women is formed to lobby on behalf of women.

1970
The first Women's Strike for Equality is held with a march in New York City and around the country, as many women refused to work that day.

Frigidaire oven advertisement,
Life magazine, February 15, 1960

This vision of a woman's role overwhelmingly applied to white women in the middle and upper classes. Poor women, especially women of color, didn't have the option of being a housewife—they had to both earn money and handle most domestic responsibilities.

Everywhere women looked, from television advertisements to women's magazines, they received the message that being a good housewife and mother was the ultimate goal of womanhood. Moreover, she was told that her happiness lay in being married and raising a family.

Many white, middle-class women tried to live up to this idealized image of womanhood. But secretly, many felt something was missing. They weren't happy at all.

CONNECT

This 1955 article titled "A Good Wife's Guide" shows society's expectations for women during this era. What might a "Good Wife or Good Husband Guide" look like today?

🔍 Avon good wife

A Woman's Work

Being a housewife may have been considered the ultimate achievement for women in the 1950s, but in truth, more women were working outside the home than ever before. Many post-World War II women had liked having a job. They wanted—and often financially needed—to continue working. Between 1940 and 1960, the number of working women doubled, and the proportion of married working mothers jumped by 400 percent.

But job ads were typically segregated by gender. The vast majority of women were limited to being secretaries, store clerks, waitresses, teachers, factory workers, or domestic help. The pay was usually low, and women had little chance of advancing to positions that paid more or offered authority.

Black women had it even worse. They earned less than their white counterparts for the same jobs, and faced racial discrimination as well as sex discrimination.

Most men refused to hire or promote women if they could place a man in the same position. Men who did have the same jobs as women were usually paid more, sometimes twice as much.

Women working in a factory in Wisconsin, 1942

Women also frequently had to endure sexual harassment and exploitation on the job. Men often hired women based on their attractiveness and felt free to make sexual suggestions to them or even touch them inappropriately. Such sexism and harassment were so commonplace that most women didn't complain. They thought it unfair, but objecting seemed pointless. Men held all the power.

WONDER WHY?

To idealize someone means representing them as perfect. Does society still idealize girls and women? If so, how? What about men? Do you feel that society pressures you to be a certain way? How so?

The Rise of Second-Wave Feminism

What finally prompted change? Several things.

For many women, the atmosphere of the Civil Rights Era awakened the possibility of a different world. With Rosa Parks refusing to rise from her bus seat and Black women playing prominent roles in the Civil Rights Movement, women of all races began to see how they could claim power.

Women became increasingly active in social justice and political issues, from the Civil Rights Movement to nuclear disarmament. As they fought these issues, they grew more indignant at the widespread discrimination and injustices they faced as women.

One of the biggest sparks prompting change came in 1963 with the book, *The Feminine Mystique.* Author Betty Friedan (1921–2006) extensively investigated the lives of white, middle-class housewives like herself. The book revealed their secret unhappiness and lack of fulfilment.

WONDER WHY?

Ever wonder what life was like for a friend, teacher, or another woman in the 1950s and 1960s? Ask her!

Vivian Malone, one of the first African Americans to attend the University of Alabama, walks through a crowd that includes photographers, National Guard members, and Deputy U.S. Attorney General Nicholas Katzenbach, 1963.

Credit: Warren K. Leffler, *U.S. News & World Report* magazine collection

🦢 WAVES OF FEMINISM 🦢

Feminism is often described as coming in waves. The first wave took place in the late nineteenth and early twentieth centuries. Feminists of that era primarily sought the right to vote and own property. Second-wave feminism arose during the mid-1960s. These women mainly focused on achieving workplace, social, and marital equality, as well as personal freedom. How many further waves of feminism have there been? What wave might we be in today?

Women across the country realized they weren't alone in wanting more from their lives than being a wife and mother. Moreover, they began to realize they had the right to pursue their own definitions of happiness. Some women started to think of themselves as feminists.

CONNECT

Has feminism left out the experiences of Black women? Many say yes, women of color have been ignored by the waves of feminism meant to make life better for all women. Take a look at this video that explains intersectionality and womenism. What do you think?

🔍 **Root feminism fails Black women**

Betty Friedan

Feminists are people who believe that women should have equal economic, social, and political rights as men. Why do you think this was such a huge change in thinking for some people?

Small Steps Forward

Although the idea of civil rights for women was still brand new, women achieved a few successes in the early 1960s. In 1963, the U.S. Congress passed the Equal Pay Act, a law that mandated equal pay for equal work, regardless of gender. The following year, Title VII of the Civil Rights Act of 1964 was enacted, prohibiting discrimination by sex (along with race and other categories) in employment.

The Civil Rights Act created the Equal Employment Opportunity Commission (EEOC), an agency designed to investigate claims of discrimination in employment, housing, and other areas. Women were hopeful that the EEOC would help end workplace gender discrimination. But, despite receiving thousands of sex discrimination claims, the agency ignored most of them. In 1965, it even ruled that sex-segregated job ads, or advertisements that specifically denied a specific gender, weren't illegal.

The Equal Pay Act wasn't proving to be very helpful either. In the mid-1960s, white women generally were still making an average of 60 cents for every dollar earned by men. Black women were making even less.

WONDER WHY?

The Declaration of Independence says Americans have the right to pursue happiness. What do you think that means? What is your definition of happiness?

President Kennedy signs the Equal Pay Act, 1963.

The Power of NOW

Frustrated feminist leaders decided to form a national women's organization that would fight for women's civil rights. In 1966, Betty Friedan came up with a name: the National Organization of Women (NOW). She would become the organization's first president.

NOW took action quickly. It waged battles in courts, lobbied politicians and agencies, and created education programs to address gender discrimination. The organization also used protests to bring attention to women's concerns.

Members of NOW, 1968

For example, in August 1967, NOW members picketed *The New York Times* offices to protest its policy of gender-segregated job ads. Later that year, the organization also mobilized women in five cities to demonstrate against the EEOC for finding such ads legal. Their pressure was successful. In 1968, the EEOC finally ruled that segregated ads were illegal.

Some feminists engaged in even more radical protests. Most famously, a few hundred women protested the Miss America beauty pageant in Atlantic City, New Jersey, in 1968. Among other things, they set up a "Freedom Trashcan" outside the pageant hall in which they threw objects they felt symbolized women's oppression, such as high heels, bras, and kitchen utensils. The protest didn't end the pageant, but it attracted nationwide attention.

☾☾ THE GENDER WAGE GAP ☽☽

You might think that society could have solved the problem of the gender wage gap by the year 2020, but it hasn't. As of 2018, white women overall earned 15 percent less than white men. That means a white woman earns 85 cents to every dollar a white man earns. And it's worse for Black women, who are paid 61 cents for every dollar a white man makes. Latinx women are paid 53 cents compared to white men. What can we do to change this?

Time for a Big Action

Despite the advances women made during the 1960s, society still didn't take women seriously. Women's protests and grievances rarely made the front pages of newspapers. Some people remained unaware of the women's liberation movement or dismissed it as an isolated group of angry women.

In March 1970, Betty Friedan called for a nationwide women's strike during a NOW conference. The strike would take place on August 26, 1970—the 50th anniversary of women winning the right to vote.

Poster by artist Juliette Gordon, 1971

PAULI MURRAY

Pauli Murray (1910–1985) was an African American lawyer, Episcopal priest, and cofounder of NOW. Her heavy involvement in the Civil Rights Movement, and particularly its legal battles against segregation, led her to advance the idea that women needed an NAACP-style organization to further their cause. Murray shattered numerous barriers as an African American and as a woman and is celebrated as a leading thinker and scholar of the Civil Rights Era.

CONNECT

Read a short biography of Murray and examine some of her poems at this website. What can poetry accomplish that other forms of protest can't?

 Poetry Foundation Murray

Friedan originally envisioned women across the country refusing to go to work or clean the house that day and instead march together in demonstration. She wanted it to be an action so big the media couldn't ignore it, and the country would see the political power of women. NOW members agreed.

Organizing a nationwide event was extremely complicated. Because women hailed from a variety of places and had such diverse ages, identities, and experiences, there was often conflict about how the protest should play out and disagreement on the issues most deserving of a spotlight.

Each NOW chapter was encouraged to rally women in its region to create their own march or demonstration.

In the end, NOW organizers decided the demonstration would focus on three demands: equal opportunities in jobs and education, free childcare centers, and access to abortions. In addition, they decided the strike would be largely symbolic. No one would pressure women to walk out on their jobs or families.

WONDER WHY?

Why might a symbolic strike send a clear message to society for a women's rights movement, but wouldn't work for a farmworkers' rights movement?

Although the city had restricted the protestors to only one lane, so many participants turned out that they filled the entire street and spilled over onto the sidewalks.

Spirits were high. Despite their differences, women felt the power of female solidarity. Demonstrators linked arms and sang, pushed their babies in strollers, chanted, and called to onlookers to join them. They carried hundreds of signs and banners with slogans such as "Don't Iron While the Strike is Hot!" and "Sisterhood is Powerful!"

Strike Day Arrives!

The turnout for the strike was a success beyond Friedan's wildest dreams. Thousands of women of all ages gathered in early evening and began marching down 5th Avenue in New York City.

Elsewhere in the city, women arrived at corporations and presented businessmen with sarcastic "Barefoot and Pregnant" awards for creating degrading images of women in their advertising and for underemploying women. Another large group headed to Liberty Island to drape a large banner over the base of the Statue of Liberty, reading "Women of the World Unite!"

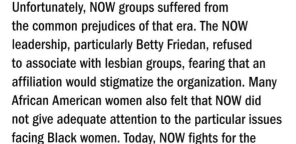

IDENTITY POLITICS

Unfortunately, NOW groups suffered from the common prejudices of that era. The NOW leadership, particularly Betty Friedan, refused to associate with lesbian groups, fearing that an affiliation would stigmatize the organization. Many African American women also felt that NOW did not give adequate attention to the particular issues facing Black women. Today, NOW fights for the issues of women of all backgrounds and identities.

Women march for equality, August 26, 1970.
Credit: *U.S. News & World Report* magazine collection, Library of Congress

Demonstrations, protests, and other pro-woman acts across the country demanded attention. An estimated 1,000 protestors marched in Washington, DC, and thousands rallied in Indianapolis, Indiana, and San Francisco, California. In Detroit, Michigan, female employees at the *Detroit Free Press* conducted a lengthy sit-in in the men's washroom because men had two washrooms and women had only one.

In other cities, women staged sit-ins in male-only bars and restaurants or participated in teach-ins about the issues women faced. Women in some offices held baby-ins and brought their babies to work to highlight the need for daycare.

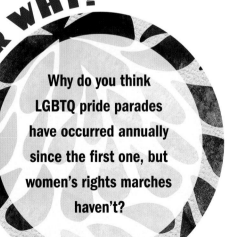

WONDER WHY?

Why do you think LGBTQ pride parades have occurred annually since the first one, but women's rights marches haven't?

> **"If I didn't define myself for myself, I would be crunched into other people's fantasies for me and eaten alive."**
>
> Audre Lorde, self-described Black, lesbian, mother, warrior, poet

Immediate Aftermath

The strike grabbed national attention as NOW had hoped. The New York City mayor, the New York governor, and President Nixon all issued announcements designating August 26 Woman's Equality Day. Women's issues, particularly the proposed Equal Rights Amendment, were in the spotlight.

After the strike, a CBS poll showed that four out of five adults were aware of women's liberation. NOW's membership quickly doubled. Many women reported feeling more empowered and less isolated.

The strike inevitably roused critics as well. Some men were disgusted or angry. A male news anchor compared the movement to "an infectious disease." Some women didn't support it either. One even proposed a National Celebration of Womanhood Day, where women would wear frilly outfits and serve their husbands breakfast in bed.

Nonetheless, the country got the message that many women weren't satisfied with their status in society and were determined to make a change. The women's liberation movement had finally made it to the mainstream.

CONNECT

You can see more statistics on women in the labor market at this website. What do you notice about trends from the 1960s to today?

🔍 **Catalyst women workforce**

🐦 THE EQUAL RIGHTS AMENDMENT 🐦

The Equal Rights Amendment (ERA) is a proposed amendment to the U.S. Constitution guaranteeing equality for all Americans, regardless of gender. The amendment passed both houses of Congress in 1972, but only 35 of 38 state legislatures ratified it before a 1979 deadline. In 2020, Virginia became the 38th state to ratify it, but its future remains uncertain.

How Far We've Come

The women's movement took off after the groundbreaking strike. Although feminists of the era didn't achieve all of their goals, there's no doubt that women's role in society had changed substantially.

According to 2018 Labor Bureau statistics, 57.1 percent of women now participate in the labor force, compared to 69 percent of men. Women are now equally represented in medical school, law school, all management jobs, and hold more professional degrees than men.

Women are also much better represented in politics. As of 2020, 101 women serve in the U.S. House of Representatives and 25 serve in the U.S. Senate. That's a far cry from 1960, when there was a total of 19 female members of Congress!

Still, there's more work to do. On average, women make 80 cents for every dollar that men earn. Affordable childcare is often hard to find. In the top 500 U.S. corporations, 95 percent of the chief executive officers are men. There has yet to be a female U.S. president. And the #MeToo movement, which began in 2006 and gained a lot of steam in 2017, shows that sexual assault and harassment of women remains common.

But there's no doubt that the future holds more waves of feminists ready and willing to tackle these problems.

As we've seen, protest was an incredibly useful tool through the Civil Rights Era, and it's still used to great effect today. Have you ever joined a climate protest? A Black Lives Matter rally? As we continue to try to improve life for everyone in society, we can count on protests being used as a way to communicate demands and pave the way for solutions.

Word Power!

What vocabulary words did you discover? Can you figure out the meanings of these words? Look in the glossary for help!

affiliation, feminist, idealize, intersectionality, mandate, sexual harassment, and stigma

Explore Intersectionality

Like most social movements, second-wave feminism had many internal conflicts about the goals for the movement. Today, many people would say these struggles were largely due to a failure to account for intersectionality.

Intersectionality refers to how the combination of a person's different identities affects their social status, power, privileges, and experience of oppression. Such identities might include race, economic status, sexual identity, religion, physical abilities, nationality, and more.

For example, a Latinx transgender woman will have different concerns and experiences of oppression than a heterosexual white woman. A deaf, working-class, Asian American woman will have different concerns and experiences than a hearing, upper-class African American woman.

The diversity of women's identities and experience meant that the groups of the 1960s had different issues and objectives, causing tension within the movement.

☮ **Draw a Venn diagram showing how being a woman can intersect with the different identities mentioned above.**

· If you were planning a women's march or demonstration today, how would you ensure that women felt all intersections of their identities were represented?

· Do you think intersectionality may have caused conflicts in any of the other movements of the Civil Rights Era? If so, which ones? How so?

TEXT TO WORLD Why is it important to have all genders represented at the highest levels of government?

Props in Protest

During the Women's Strike for Equality, women used creativity to draw attention to the problems they faced. In Boston, a woman chained herself to an enormous paper typewriter during a march. In San Francisco, women attached pots and pans to their backs. At the Miss American pageant, protestors created "Freedom Trashcans" to throw away symbols of female oppression.

☮ **Consider a problem or issue that you care about.** What props could you use to make a statement in protest?

☮ **Create a prop representing the issue.** As you design your prop, think about these questions.

- What is the problem that you want to highlight?
- How does the prop relate to or showcase the problem?
- How does your prop make people think about the problem?
- Can people interact with the prop?
- Does the prop clearly communicate the message or does it leave people guessing?

The Women's Strike for Equality helped pave the way for the Women's March of 2017, when an estimated 4 million women worldwide marched in response to the perceived threat U.S. President Donald Trump's administration presented to women's, civil, and human rights.

abolish: to completely do away with something.

abortion: the intentional ending of pregnancy.

activist: a person who fights for something they believe in.

advocate: a person who publicly supports a particular cause or policy.

affiliation: a connection to something.

assassinate: to murder an important person for political or religious reasons.

backlash: a strong, negative reaction by a large group of people to a social or political event.

bail: a sum of money given to be temporarily released from jail. It is to guarantee that person's appearance in court.

bisexual: sexually attracted to both men and women.

Black Lives Matter: a protest movement founded to defeat white supremacy and build local power to intervene in violence inflicted on Black communities by the state and individuals.

blackface: the practice of painting one's face dark to mimic a Black person, recognized as racist.

blackmail: an illegal act in which someone demands money from a person in return for not revealing information about that person that would be damaging.

boycott: to refuse to buy certain goods or use certain services as a form of protest.

brutality: great physical and mental cruelty.

capitalism: an economy in which people, not the government, own the factories, ships, and land used in the production and distribution of goods.

citizen: a person who has all the rights and responsibilities that come with being a full member of a country.

civil disobedience: refusing to obey certain laws or pay taxes as a peaceful form of political protest.

Civil Rights Movement: a national movement for racial equality in the 1950s and 1960s.

civil rights: the basic rights that all citizens of a society are supposed to have, such as the right to vote.

clientele: customers.

Cold War: a rivalry between the Soviet Union and the United States that began after World War II.

colonize: to take control of an area and the people who live there.

commissioner: a person in charge of a certain department or district.

communist: a political system controlled by a single party that believes the wealth of the country should be owned by everyone and shared evenly.

condone: to accept and agree with something.

confiscate: when someone in authority seizes a possession.

conscience: a person's beliefs about what is morally right.

conscientious objector: a person who refuses to serve in a military conflict or carry weapons for moral or religious reasons.

conscription: the drafting of men into military service.

constitutionality: aligned with the principles set forth in the U.S. Constitution.

contemporary: existing at the same time as something else.

conventional: ordinary.

cultivate: to prepare and use land for growing food. To encourage something to grow and expand.

culture: a group of people and their beliefs and way of life.

custom: a way of living and doing things, such as food and dress.

deferment: a temporary delay in taking someone in the military forces.

democracy: a form of government in which all people can vote for representatives.

deport: to expel a person from a country.

derogatory: unkind actions or words intended to express a low opinion of someone.

desegregate: to end segregation of people according to racial, religious, or other differences.

dictator: a person who rules with complete authority, often in a brutal or cruel manner.

discrimination: the unjust treatment of some groups of people based on such things as race, religion, gender, or something else.

dispatch: to send something or do an action.

dissent: to disagree with a widely held opinion.

domestic: related to the running of a home or family.

draft: a government requirement that men join the military.

drag: a performance in which the performers wear clothing more conventionally worn by another gender.

economic: having to do with the resources and wealth of a country.

empower: to give someone authority and power.

estranged: to be alienated from an individual or a group.

ethical: acting in a way that upholds someone's belief in right and wrong.

exclude: to keep out.

exemption: freedom from an obligation.

exploit: to benefit unfairly from someone else's work.

fasting: not eating or drinking by choice for a period of time, for example as part of a religious ritual or as an act of protest.

feminist: a person who believes men and women should have equal rights and opportunities.

foreign policy: the way the government deals with other nations.

galvanize: to strengthen.

garment: cloth goods, such as clothes.

gay: sexually attracted to people of the same sex. This word is usually used to describe men, but may be used to describe women.

gender: the behavioral, cultural, or psychological traits typically associated with masculinity and femininity.

gender identity: a person's internal sense of being male, female, some combination of male and female, or neither male nor female.

grievance: a cause for complaint or protest, especially when it has to do with being treated unfairly.

harassment: aggressive pressure or intimidation.

heterosexual: a person who is sexually attracted to people of the opposite gender.

homosexual: a person who is sexually attracted to others of the same gender.

iconic: describes something that is famous for or symbolizes an idea, group of things, or period of time.

idealize: to represent as perfect.

immigrant: a person who comes into a country to live permanently.

immoral: not conforming to accepted standards of morality.

inauguration: a ceremony or celebration to introduce a person or thing.

indefinitely: having no clearly defined boundaries.

induction: an occasion when someone is formally introduced to a new job or organization.

inequality: differences in opportunity and treatment based on social, ethnic, racial, or economic qualities.

inevitable: unable to be avoided.

inferior: lower in rank or status or quality.

initiate: to start a process.

injustice: something that is very unfair or unequal.

integrate: to bring different races together.

intercept: to prevent something from continuing to a destination.

intersectionality: the interconnected nature of certain identities, such as race, class, and gender, especially as they relate to civil rights.

intimidate: to make someone fearful.

invisibility: to be unseen or unnoticed.

isolate: to be separate from others.

Jim Crow: the legally enforced discrimination of Black people that led to the practice of segregating African Americans in the United States.

jubilant: feeling great happiness and triumph.

Ku Klux Klan (KKK): a terrorist group formed after the Civil War that believes white Christians should hold the power in society.

labor union: a group of workers that bargains with the people they work for.

legacy: something handed down from the past that has a long-lasting impact.

legislation: the act of making new laws.

legislature: a government body that creates laws.

legitimize: to make something acceptable or legal.

lesbian: a woman who is sexually attracted to women.

LGBTQ: stands for lesbian, gay, bisexual, transgender, and queer.

loophole: an error in a law that makes it possible for some people to legally disobey it.

lottery: a random selection.

Mafia: a powerful crime organization.

mandate: an authoritative command or instruction.

marginalized: treated as insignificant or unimportant.

meager: very little, not nearly enough.

#MeToo: a movement against sexual harassment where people publicly accuse offenders.

migrant: a person who moves from one place to another to find work or better living or work conditions.

militant: combative and aggressive in support of a political or social cause.

minstrel: a traveling musician or an entertainer in a variety show.

moral: ethical and honest behavior.

motivate: to give someone reason to do something.

NAACP: the National Association for the Advancement of Colored People, a group formed during the early twentieth century to advance justice for African Americans.

national security: a term describing the defense and protection of the interests of a country.

neutralize: to stop something from having an effect.

nonbinary: gender identities that are not exclusively masculine or feminine.

nonviolent protest: the practice of achieving goals such as social change through symbolic protests, civil disobedience, economic noncooperation, or other methods, all while being nonviolent.

nuclear disarmament: the act of reducing or eliminating nuclear weapons.

oppress: to use unjust or cruel authority and power to persecute someone.

ostracize: to exclude from a group.

pacifist: a person who is opposed to war or violence.

patriotic: a feeling of devotion to and love for one's country.

pesticide: a chemical used to kill pests on crops.

picket: to stand or march near a certain place to protest or persuade others not to enter.

plight: a dangerous, difficult, or unfortunate situation.

pre-induction: an informational program for people joining the military.

prejudice: having an unfair or unfavorable opinion or feeling about a person or group, usually formed without knowledge, thought, or reason.

privilege: a right or benefit that is given to some people but not to others.

profits: the amount of money made after deducting expenses.

prominent: important.

protest: a statement or action expressing disapproval of or objection to something.

racism: negative opinions or treatment of people based on race and the notion that people of a different race are inferior because of their race.

racist: hatred of people of a different race.

radical: a person with extreme political or social views.

recruit: to enlist new people to a cause or army.

reform: the improvement of wrong or bad conditions.

regime: a government or system, especially one that has firm control over people.

repatriation: the return of someone to their own country.

retaliation: fighting back in response to an attack.

revolt: to fight against a government or person of authority.

scapegoat: someone or something blamed for a failure.

segregation: the enforced separation of different racial groups in a community or country.

sexual harassment: harassment involving the making of unwanted sexual advances or inappropriate remarks.

sexual orientation: a person's sexual identity in relation to the gender to which they are attracted.

slave: a person considered the legal property of another and forced to work without pay, against their will.

slogan: a catchy saying such as those used in advertisements.

social justice: the fair distribution of wealth, opportunities, and privileges within a society.

Soviet Union: a communist country that existed from 1922 until 1991 that included present-day Russia.

status quo: the current state of things.

stigma: a mark of shame or discredit.

strike: an organized protest in which people refuse to work until changes are made in the workplace.

suffrage: the right to vote in political elections.

sustain: to keep something going.

symbol: a physical representation of a thing or idea.

syndicate: an organization.

totalitarian: a system of government that has absolute control over its people and requires them to be completely obedient.

traitor: a person who is not loyal to their country, social groups, or own beliefs.

transgender: a person whose actual gender differs from the gender they were assigned at birth.

transgression: an act that goes against laws or rules.

unconstitutional: not in agreement or accordance with a political constitution, especially the U.S. Constitution.

underprivileged: to have few opportunities or resources.

unequivocal: leaving no doubt.

union: a group that represents workers when dealing with the employer.

vandalize: to deliberately destroy or damage property.

white supremacy: the racist belief that white people are superior to those of all other races and should therefore dominate society.

RESOURCES

BOOKS

Bausum, Ann. *Stonewall: Breaking Out in the Fight for Gay Rights.* Speak, 2016.

Cavallo, Francesca, and Elena Favilli. *Good Night Stories for Rebel Girls: 100 Tales of Extraordinary Women.* Rebel Girls, 2016.

Dearman, Jill. *Feminism: The March Toward Equal Rights for Women.* Nomad Press, 2019.

Diggs, Barbara. *The Vietnam War.* Nomad Press, 2018.

Hoose, Phillip. *Claudette Colvin: Twice Toward Justice.* Square Fish, 2010.

Jennings, Jazz. *Being Jazz: My Life as a (Transgender) Teen.* Ember, 2017.

Jensen, Kelly, ed. *Here We Are: Feminism for the Real World.* Algonquin Young Readers, 2017.

MUSEUMS

The National Civil Rights Museum at the Lorraine Motel, Memphis, Tennessee: civilrightsmuseum.org

The National Center for Civil and Human Rights in Atlanta, Georgia: civilandhumanrights.org

The GLBT Historical Society Museum in San Francisco, California: glbthistory.org/museum-about-visitor-info

WEBSITES

Cesar Chavez Foundation: chavezfoundation.org/national-chavez-center

"City of Workers, City of Struggle" exhibit: mcny.org/exhibition/city-workers-city-struggle

QR CODE GLOSSARY

PAGE 3: vermont.pbslearningmedia.org/resource/americon-vid-rosa-parks/video

PAGE 6: davidrugglescenter.org

PAGE 11: ferris.edu/HTMLS/news/jimcrow/links/misclink/examples.htm

PAGE 11: people.howstuffworks.com/jane-elliott.htm

PAGE 20: npr.org/templates/story/story.php?storyId=1304163

PAGE 21: news.berkeley.edu/2020/02/11/podcast-montgomery-bus-boycott-womens-political-council

PAGE 24: atlasobscura.com/articles/who-funded-civil-rights-movement

PAGE 29: youtube.com/watch?v=NpY2NVcO17U

PAGE 34: archive.org/details/CEP531

PAGE 39: youtube.com/watch?v=tFFOUkipl4U

PAGE 41: youtube.com/watch?v=aS3-HdthMVo

PAGE 47: mtsu.edu/first-amendment/article/709/united-states-v-o-brien

RESOURCES

QR CODE GLOSSARY (CONTINUED)

PAGE 51: washingtonpost.com/news/retropolis/wp/2018/08/13/the-time-a-president-deported-1-million-mexican-americans-for-stealing-u-s-jobs

PAGE 51: pbs.org/ancestorsintheamericas/time_21.html

PAGE 52: youtube.com/watch?v=yJTVF_dya7E

PAGE 55: npca.org/articles/1555-remembering-the-manongs-and-story-of-the-filipino-farm-worker-movement

PAGE 65: youtube.com/watch?v=tXan6Sw_okc

PAGE 71: theguardian.com/lifeandstyle/2019/jun/19/stonewall-50th-anniversary-night-that-unleashed-gay-liberation

PAGE 77: euronews.com/2019/06/28/why-is-lgbt-pride-day-celebrated-on-june-28

PAGE 79: news.gallup.com/poll/1651/gay-lesbian-rights.aspx

PAGE 81: youtube.com/watch?v=V2trZ2wWW5w

PAGE 86: avconline.avc.edu/bbeyer/Bb_WIO_Articles/Ch3_A/GoodWifesGuide_1955.pdf

PAGE 89: youtube.com/watch?v=t9KMtf_e_ew

PAGE 92: poetryfoundation.org/poets/pauli-murray

PAGE 95: catalyst.org/research/women-in-the-workforce-united-states

SELECTED BIBLIOGRAPHY

Appy, Christian G. *American Reckoning: The Vietnam War and Our National Identity.* Viking, 2016.

Branch, Taylor. *The King Years: Historic Moments in the Civil Rights Movement.* Simon & Schuster, 2013.

Brill, Marlene Targ. *Dolores Huerta Stands Strong: The Woman Who Demanded Justice.* Ohio University Press, 2018.

Foley, Michael Stewart. *Confronting the War Machine: Draft Resistance during the Vietnam War.* University of North Carolina Press, 2003.

King Jr., Martin Luther. *Stride Toward Freedom: The Montgomery Story.* Harper & Brothers, 1958.

Pitman, Gayle E. *The Stonewall Riots: Coming Out in the Streets.* Abrams Books, 2019.

Rau, Dana Meachen. *Who Was Cesar Chavez?* Penguin Random House LLC, 2017.

Rosen, Ruth. *The World Split Open: How the Modern Women's Movement Changed America.* Viking, 2000.